W9-BQY-406

SUICIDE
BEHIND
| B | A | R | S |

SUICIDE
BEHIND
| B | A | R | S |
Prediction and Prevention

David Lester, PhD & Bruce L. Danto, MD

The Charles Press, Publishers
Philadelphia

Copyright © 1993 by The Charles Press, Publishers, Inc.

The Charles Press, Publishers
Post Office Box 15715
Philadelphia, PA 19103

Library of Congress Cataloging-in-Publication Data

Lester, David, 1942-

   Suicide Behind Bars: prediction and prevention / David Lester and
Bruce L. Danto.

      p.   cm.
   Includes bibliographical references.
   ISBN 0-914783-62-9
   1. Prisoners—United States—Suicidal behavior. 2. Prisoners-Europe—
Suicidal behavior. 3. Suicide—Prevention.   I. Danto,
Bruce L. II. Title.
HV6545.6.L47 1992
365'.6—dc20

                                    92-27480
                                    CIP

ISBN 0-914783-62-9

Printed in the United States of America

Contents

Introduction

The primary aim of this book is to provide a useable knowledge of suicide and its prevention for those involved in the criminal justice system, particularly personnel in correctional facilities. The need for this information is clear: suicide among those who are incarcerated is very high compared to other groups in society. In fact, suicide is now among the leading causes of death in correctional institutions in the United States, especially in jails and detention centers. Approximately 30 percent of all deaths of inmates in larger jails (those with more than 100 inmates) are the result of suicide and it is estimated that the suicide rate in detention and holding cells is *nine* times greater than in the general population.

Suicide in prison is particularly difficult to accept because, in addition to the tragic and needless loss of lives, it occurs in a presumably protected environment — behind bars — with professional staff nearby. This does not mean that every inmate suicide can be prevented, but it does imply that a concerted effort must be made in every correctional institution to achieve this goal. If not, the inmate suicide rate will continue to increase and with it the number of lawsuits that are filed by the families of the deceased. Understandably, families are usually convinced that a suicide could have been prevented, and they demand, and more often than not, receive large sums of money from the institutions they sue. In other words, suicide prevention in custody is more than an ethical and moral issue, it is now also a legal battleground.

Toward this end, it is mandatory that all correctional workers including administrative staffs possess a fundamental understanding of suicide, focusing on these key questions: who commits suicide, why do they kill themselves, how can high-risk candidates be identified, and what measures can be taken to prevent suicide?

Throughout this book we have made the deliberate effort to distinguish between lockups, jails and prisons. The reason for this delineation is that those who commit suicide in these different types of facilities have significantly different characteristics and therefore cannot be considered as a single population. Also, each type of facility usually represents a different stage of the incarceration process (from initial arrest to long-term stay) and each prisoner's response varies with these different levels of confinement. Correctional officers should be aware of this because different prevention strategies are necessary at each type of institution. The terms used in this book are defined as follows:

Lockup: A holding facility, located in a police station, that maintains custody of a detainee for less than 24 hours.

Jail: A penal institution that holds those who have been arrested and are either being held for further investigation or are awaiting trial. Some jails also hold inmates who will be or already have been convicted of a crime. These facilities are run by local city or county governments.

Prison: A facility operated by the state or federal government that confines felons who generally have been sentenced to one year or more.

Correctional Facilities: This term is used here to refer to jails and prisons collectively.

Before beginning this presentation it may be helpful to clarify another issue in this book. Suicide prediction and many other aspects of suicide are by no means an exact science at this stage and much of what we know about suicide is subject to debate. For this reason, rather that using a dogmatic approach, we have presented the evidence for each issue so that the reader can appreciate both sides of the story. This will explain the many research studies described, especially those in the early chapters.

It is our hope that the information we have presented in this book will help all of those in the criminal justice system to identify at-risk inmates, to intervene and prevent unnecessary deaths. The ultimate goal is to reverse the trend of suicide behind bars from an escalating tragedy to a rare occurrence.

Chapter 1

The Spectrum of Inmate Suicide

Each suicide is unique and represents in effect a drama that unfolds before the eyes of a correctional or police officer. Although each case is different there are many similarities that may alert the prepared officer to impending trouble. Sometimes, but not always, the officer may be able to anticipate the suicidal act and prevent it by the way he handles the situation. On other occasions, however, he misses the opportunity or fails in his effort. Each of the following brief case histories illustrates a suicide that occurred in custody and provides a picture of the different types of people who, for various reasons, chose this way out.

SEVEN CASE HISTORIES

Case 1

A 17-year-old, honor-list high school student was arrested for driving under the influence of alcohol in a small midwestern town. One of four girls in the back seat threw a beer bottle out of the window. Their littering and erratic driving was observed by a policeman. When arrested, the male passenger in the front seat became nervous and vomited.

After the six teens were taken to the police station, the investigating officer (while checking the car for possible beer bottles or drugs) found some vomit on the sleeve of his shirt. Before interrogating the driver, the officer removed his shirt and gun belt and left them on a chair in the interrogation office. In the middle of questioning the driver, the policeman was called from the room to talk to some of the parents of the teens, leaving the young man alone. Suddenly a single shot was heard. Finding himself alone with the policeman's gun, the boy shot himself once in the head and killed himself. His suicide ended up destroying the boy's parents' marriage. They filed a lawsuit against the city and won easily, settling out of court for half a million dollars.

In this case the officer erred by not appreciating the impact that an arrest for drunk driving might have on a basically good boy who was also a high achiever. Perhaps this was the boys first arrest and the shock of the experience coupled with the fact that he was probably intoxicated were factors that overwhelmed him. While the officer could not have anticipated that the boy would kill himself, he erred seriously in not maintaining control of his weapon.

Case 2

A 31-year-old male, a known drug abuser with a chronic history of arrests for fighting and intoxication, was booked into the lockup of a small suburban jail located near a large city in the Midwest. The man had been severely beaten: his back showed the imprint of a gun handle; he had a large swelling over his left kidney; coin-sized imprints across his back; and abrasions above his left collar bone and below each knee cap. The booking record did not contain this information and it was not until after his death that it was discovered that this severe beating had been delivered by the police.

As he was being escorted from the booking area to a cellblock on the second floor by two officers and the watch commander — a most unusual fact in itself — the man was over-heard by the officers and other inmates telling his wife and daughter good-bye and that he loved them. It was also later discovered that he had mentioned committing suicide while he was being booked — an indication that he should have been immediately considered by those in charge as a suicide risk. Instead of being placed in a cell across from the observation window, the man was put in a cell that was furthest away from supervision and monitoring. After locking the man in the cell the officer was called away to type a police report, an assignment that took him a long time. His return to the inmate area was seriously delayed and when he did return, he found the man dead — hanging in his cell. None of the officers present knew how to perform CPR, and so resuscitation was not even attempted.

The estate sued the city and was awarded hundreds of thousands of dollars. The jury decided that the prisoner had been abused and that his civil rights had been violated. The jail's screening program as well as its training, supervision and internal affairs investigation system, and written policies and procedures were all found to be defective. Clearly, its monitoring program was totally ineffective. Even worse, the booking officer was aware of the suicide risk since the inmate had made such a threat in front of him.

Case 3

In a northwestern state a young man encountered a snowstorm as he drove from his office to a distant town. For reasons perhaps caused by his psychiatric problems, together with the stress of driving in a snowstorm, the man developed a sense of helplessness and confusion. He parked outside of a hospital and made a phone call to his father asking for help because he was confused and did not know what to do. His father told him that he would send his brother to be with him and that he should wait at the hospital for him. So he sat and waited. The desk receptionist observed the young man sitting in the snow without a coat during the blizzard and decided to call the police.

The police officer who responded to the call accused him of being on drugs and therefore took him away to the small local jail. At the prisoner's request the officer called the boy's father who informed him of the boy's psychiatric history. Unconcerned with this information, the officer told the boy's father that he was going to hold the young man on suspicion of drug possession. The young man was placed in a cell without being booked or charged with any crime. At that time a traffic accident was reported and because he was the only one on duty, the officer left the man alone in the cell for the rest of the evening. The prisoner was frightened and begged the officer not to lock him up. The officer did not return that evening. When shifts changed the replacement officers discovered the prisoner was dead; he had hanged himself by his shoelaces. Graffiti that he had drawn on the cell wall showed a person hanging by a noose. Over the drawing were scribbled the words "High Justice."

The case was settled out of court for a huge sum of money. The lawyers agreed that there were no screening or monitoring procedures whatsoever at this jail and that no formal charges had ever been made. Not only should the officer have probably taken the frightened man to a hospital for a psychiatric examination—in light of the fact that he had a history of psychiatric problems, but he made matters worse by locking him up without charging him with a crime and not bothering to remove his shoelaces. In addition to both of these errors, he left him alone in the jail all evening; these were inexcusable mistakes.

Case 4

In a large West Coast jail, a 24-year-old married man was booked following arrest for driving his motorcycle while intoxicated. Personal bail was arranged, and he waited in a cell in the booking reception area for his wife to come and pay his bail. A young deputy was assigned to watch the man since he appeared to the booking officer to be very depressed. As the officer watched, the man rose from the cot on which he was seated and went into the bathroom. Shortly thereafter he returned to his cot. Another officer asked the deputy who was watching to assist him with some task. As he left his station, he noticed the inmate removing his T-shirt. A few minutes later a female deputy walked by and observed the inmate sitting on the cot with his head down between his knees, a posture that was understood as a sign of depression. Twenty minutes later, the original deputy returned to his station and found his prisoner hanging from his T-shirt.

There was clearly a breakdown in monitoring and a failure to obtain a mental health assessment in light of the man's obvious depression. This case illustrates how vigilance is necessary even when a prisoner is scheduled for release. If depression does not seem to be lifted when news of discharge is given, appropriate care and observation are necessary. The booking officer attributed the man's drinking to the fact that he had recently lost his job. Clearly, release from jail would not correct the problem about which he was upset.

Case 5

In a West Coast community, after smoking "crack," a 34-year-old man developed a toxic psychosis that caused hallucinations and paranoid delusions. He heard the voice of his daughter calling. He phoned her but he was so confused he could not recognize her voice. He entered his mother's room at 3:00 a.m., holding a knife in one hand and a razor in the other, and threatened to cut his wrists. His mother was able to calm him down and get him to drop his weapons. His sister called the police and stated that her brother and the family wanted him to be admitted to a psychiatric hospital. Sheriff's deputies arrived and obtained his history. When they ran a police check they discovered that he had an outstanding traffic warrant and decided to take him to jail instead of a psychiatric hospital.

The booking officer noted the history and added that he thought the man was a homosexual. He requested a mental health evaluation because he felt that the man was mentally ill and suicidal. A call was made to summon a nurse to evaluate him, but apparently she did not feel that there was any urgency to this request; she made other rounds first and these delayed her for a long time. During this time the man claimed that he was being gassed through the vents in his cell and complained of loud noise when in fact he was in a completely quiet area. These were clear signals that something was seriously wrong.

Two hours later when the nurse appeared, she saw the man lying on his cot and because she assumed he was asleep, she did not awaken him or schedule a watch so she could be notified when he awoke. Forty-five minutes later he was found hanging in his cell.

In this case the police were duly warned of the man's illness, and he should have been given a mental evaluation prior to booking. Referral resources through the nurse had broken down, and monitoring was inappropriate given his condition. In the court case against the county the award was several million dollars.

Case 6

In a southeastern state, a 30-year-old male approached a patrol car and requested that the officers take him to a mental hospital as he had a history of mental illness. From the local police station he was transferred to a county jail. It became apparent to him that he was not going to be taken to a psychiatric facility. In the second facility he lost control and assaulted an officer. This action brought about his arrest. The officer who transferred him from the first police station knew of his psychiatric history but failed to notify those in the county jail. He also fought with other inmates. The injuries he sustained in the fights were evaluated at a nearby hospital, and he was then returned to the county jail. No one made any request for a psychiatric consultation. Within an hour following his return to the jail he was found hanging by a belt in the isolation cell in which he had been placed. No monitoring of any kind had been undertaken in this jail.

This case was settled out of court for over a half a million dollars. All three police agencies involved had violated their own policies and procedures regarding the need to take a mentally ill person for medical and psychiatric screening and to insure 15-minute monitoring. The officers were not provided with training about how to deal with mentally ill persons, and there was no psychiatric screening at the time of booking.

Case 7

A man with a known history of schizophrenia and psychiatric hospitalization committed a crime and was sentenced to a maximum security prison. After he arrived, he would not get out of bed, smeared himself with feces and was totally uncommunicative. He cut his wrists and attempted to jump from the fourth level of his cellblock. He was referred to the prison psychiatrist who believed that the inmate was being manipulative and that his behavior was caused by a personality defect. He was transferred to a state forensic center for further diagnostic study where he was again diagnosed as being a faker and having a personality disorder.

Following his return to prison, the man was observed sitting on the guard rail outside his cell. He smiled at some nearby inmates and fell over backwards, plunging many feet to the floor. He died of massive brain damage.

What is significant about this case is that the correctional staff followed proper procedure and sought the medical and psychiatric consultation that the inmate's behavior required. The psychiatric staff, however, erred significantly. They did not understand the inmate's behavior, they disregarded his previous psychiatric history and the clues that he was suicidal. The psychiatric staff was sued for malpractice.

DISCUSSION

The above described cases illustrate the wide spectrum of reasons that people commit suicide. Clearly, in each case the person had his own reasons for choosing this way out and each suicide occurred under unique circumstances and conditions. The similarities in these cases are that each suicide occurred in a detention center or jail and during or shortly after booking and that the correctional or police officer failed to identify and prevent the suicidal action. This is not to say that all cases of suicide committed in custody are always a result of staff error or that inmate suicides are always preventable. Some suicides will occur no matter how well designed the prevention system is and how carefully procedures are carried out.

But, as in the above cases, there are often serious flaws in the system. Some of these problems that will be discussed in later chapters are: far too many institutions do not have organized suicide prevention programs; only a limited number of correctional and police officers are trained sufficiently to identify high-risk inmates and act effectively in preventing suicide; and the risk of suicide, particularly shortly after arrest, is grossly underestimated.

Chapter 2

Inmate Suicide: How Common Is It?

Although we shall see later that it is very difficult to predict the suicidal behavior of *individuals*, the suicide rates in *society* as a whole and of groups within society remain quite stable and predictable. For example, the suicide rate in the United States has remained steady at approximately 10 to 12 per 100,000 per year since 1950 (Lester 1989a). The suicide rate of men in America is about three to four times higher than the suicide rate of women, and the suicide rate of whites is about twice the suicide rate of African Americans.

The stability in societal suicide rates has enabled sociologists to devise reliable theories to account for social suicide rates. The first of these theories was proposed by Emile Durkheim in 1897; his theory is still influential today.

THEORIES OF THE SOCIETAL SUICIDE RATE

Durkheim's Theory of Suicide

Durkheim proposed that two characteristics of a society affected its suicide rate. First, the level of social integration in a society was associated with the suicide rate. Sociologists have disagreed on how exactly to define social integration, but it can safely be understood as the degree to which people have social relationships with the other people in society. Durkheim suggested that when suicides are committed because a person is too weakly integrated that these should be called *egoistic* suicides, as in the case of an isolated person living alone in a rooming house in a deteriorated section of a city. Much less common are suicides committed because the person is too strongly integrated into the society. These are called *altruistic* suicides, as when a soldier throws himself onto an live hand grenade in order to save a fellow soldier.

The second social characteristic proposed by Durkheim for explaining societal suicide rates was social regulation, in other words, the degree to which a person's desires are controlled by society. Suicides committed because this regulation is too weak are called *anomic* suicides, as in the case of an alienated adolescent who feels despair that his desires can never be gratified by society. Suicides committed because a person's degree of social regulation is too strong are called *fatalistic* suicides, as when people who are totally regulated by society kill themselves as a way of escaping from the bonds of society, as some slaves may have done.

Modern sociologists have argued that altruistic and fatalistic suicides are rare in modern society and that suicide is more common when social integration and social regulation are too weak. However, it may be that prisons constitute a deviant type of society where social regulation may be unduly high. Thus, some prison suicides may be fatalistic in nature.

Henry and Short's Theory of Suicide

Henry and Short (1954) focused on the degree to which people's behaviors in the society are constrained or restrained by others. For example, consider the oppressed in a society, as in the case of blacks in South Africa. When their life is miserable, they have obvious external sources to blame for their misery. Therefore, anger is justified and they are more likely to be assaultive than depressed. As a consequence, the extreme behavior of murder will be relatively more common. In contrast, the oppressors in the society, for example, the white Afrikaners in South Africa, have fewer obvious external sources to blame for their misery. Thus, they are more likely to become depressed and, in the extreme, suicidal. In support of this, Lester (1989b) has noted that blacks in South Africa have higher rates of homicide, while whites have higher rates of suicide.

Lester's Social Deviancy Theory of Suicide

Lester (1989c) has suggested that people who fit in with the general characteristics of the community will be less likely to feel stress and so will be less likely to commit suicide than those who do not fit in. For example, whereas adult married people have low suicide rates (most adults are married and most married people are adults), married teenagers have a relatively higher suicide rate (few teenagers are married and few married people are teenagers).

THE INCIDENCE OF SUICIDE IN INMATES

Underreporting Suicides

Before presenting data on the suicide of inmates, it must be borne in mind that official suicide statistics for the general population are often criticized for being inaccurate. By looking at medical examiner records it is easy to document that many if not most suicides are often misclassified in the official records. For example, Hlady and Middaugh (1988) examined 3924 deaths in Alaska and found that 193 of them were suicides; of these, only 141 were actually recorded as suicides by the state and 112 by the federal government. The underrating was greater for the suicides of native Americans. The omissions by the government were typically due to delayed determinations, a failure to update records and sometimes erroneous certification.

Such misclassification probably also occurs for prisoners. For example, Smith (1984) documented a suicide in an English prison that he thought was a coverup of a murder committed by the guards. Hayes (1989) examined the deaths of inmates of Ohio penal institutions during 1981-1982; the prison records reported that there had been 22 suicides, but Hayes discovered that 46 of the deaths were almost certainly suicides. It is not hard to imagine all sorts of reasons why suicides committed in custody might be covered up by the prison in question and by the county and state responsible for that prison.

Consequently, we must expect that reported suicide rates for inmates will be underestimated, and that they could very possibly be greater underestimates than those that are given for the general population. There is a greater demand for accurate certification of death of non-inmates (Haycock 1991a, 1991b).

Inmate Suicides as a Percentage of Deaths

There have been several studies of the percentage of deaths of inmates due to suicide, a percentage that for the general population in 1988 was 1.4 percent, for all American males was 2.1 percent, and for males aged 20 to 29, 14.4 percent.

Frost and Hanzlick (1988) identified 53 deaths over an 11-year period in the Atlanta and Fulton County jails, of which 14 (26 percent) were suicides, 8 were accidental, 2 were homicides and 29 were natural deaths. Copeland (1984) counted 229 prisoner deaths in Dade County (Greater Miami) from 1956 to 1982, of which 21 percent were suicides. Adelson and co-workers (1968) found 91 prisoner deaths in Cuyahoga County (Cleveland) from 1956 to 1967, of which 23 (25 percent) were from suicide. This percentage was similar for both white prisoners (26 percent) and black prisoners (24 percent).

Lanphear (1987) identified 33 deaths in a county detention center in Tennessee over a 15-year period. Of these, 23 were natural deaths, 6 were accidents, and 8 were suicides. The percentage of deaths due to suicide was, therefore, 23 percent.

All of these estimates for the percentage of suicide deaths in county jails are in the area of 21 to 26 percent. The only deviant reports come from Smialek and Spitz (1978), who reported that 80 percent of prisoner deaths (20 of 25) in the Wayne County (Detroit) jails in 1976 to 1977 were from suicide, and from Novick and Remmlinger (1978), who found that 41 percent of the deaths in New York City correctional facilities from 1971 to 1976 were from suicide.

In the Maryland state prison system from 1979 to 1987, 18 percent of the deaths were suicides (Salive et al. 1989). In Tennessee, Jones (1976) found that 19 percent of prison deaths from 1972 to 1973 were from suicide.

Niemi (1978) reported that 32 percent of the deaths that occurred in lockups in Finland from 1963 to 1967 were from suicide, and Pounder (1986) found that 32 percent of the deaths in an Australian prison from 1973 to 1983 were from suicide. In Scotland, suicides accounted for 37 percent of the deaths from 1970 to 1982 (Backett 1987). However, in Denmark from 1981 to 1985, Segest (1987) found zero percent of the deaths that occurred while in police custody were from suicide!

The Rate of Suicide: Jails

In 1985, the rate of suicide for the entire general population in the United States was 12.3 per 100,000 per year (19.9 were men and 5.1 were women); rising from 10.0 for those aged 15 to 19 to 25.3 for those aged 80 to 84; and ranging in 1980 from 7.4 in

New Jersey to 22.9 in Nevada (Lester 1989a). What are the suicide rates for prisoners and how do they compare to the rest of the population?

Basing their calculations on the average daily prison population, Frost and Hanzlick (1988) calculated a suicide rate of 114 per 100,000 per year for the Atlanta and Fulton County jails from 1974 to 1985. Copeland (1989) studied all correctional facilities in Dade County, Florida, from 1978 to 1988 and found a suicide rate of 47 per 100,000 per year. In six midwestern jails, between the years 1966 and 1971, Esparza (1973) calculated a suicide rate of 58. Novick and Remmlinger (1978) found a suicide rate of 96 in all New York City correctional facilities between 1971 and 1976.

For the U.S. as a whole, Winfree (1988) calculated the suicide rates in jails in 1977 and 1982 to be 187.5 and 131.5, respectively — much higher than for people in the general population of similar age, sex and race (22.6 and 21.7, respectively). Hayes (1989) calculated a suicide rate of 107 for detention facilities in the U.S. in 1986, but was not able to calculate a suicide rate for holding facilities because of the lack of a reliable estimate of the daily population in holding facilities. It can be seen that almost all of the suicide rates reported for jails are very high.

The Rate of Suicide: Prisons

Anno (1985) calculated a suicide rate of 18.6 for sentenced prisoners in the Texas Department of Corrections from 1980 to 1985. Stone (1984) reported a suicide rate of 137.5 in Texas jails in 1981. For prisons he reported a suicide rate of 15.9. Salive and associates (1989) calculated that the suicide rates of prisoners with sentences of over one year in the Maryland state prisons were 39.6 for men, 0.0 for women and 63.1 for whites, 30.9 for blacks. The age range with the highest suicide rate was 25 to 34 years, with a rate of 52.4; the crime with the highest suicide rate was murder, with a rate of 91.2; the sentence with the peak suicide rate was life, with a rate of 146.0; and the rate was higher in the maximum security institutions where the rate was 131.5. The suicide rates for white and black male inmates were higher than for men of the same age in the community.

In a Marion County, Oregon, prison, from 1983 to 1987, Batten (1989) reported a suicide rate of 820 per 100,000 per year for forensic psychiatric patients (offenders with severe psychiatric disturbances and psychiatric patients who present management problems), as compared to a rate of 289 suicides for general psychiatric patients. The state correctional facilities had a suicide rate of 29 — not unduly high for males in Oregon.

Haycock (1991c) noted that an institution for the criminally insane in Massachusetts had a relatively high suicide rate from 1886 to 1989, whereas the institutions for defective delinquents, those considered to be sexually dangerous and the offenders who were drug addicts had relatively low suicide rates.

Payson (1975) informally surveyed 45 states and estimated a suicide rate of 36 for state prisoners in 1972. The suicide rate did not differ much at all between the ten most populous states and the ten least populous states (33 versus 34).

Rieger (1971) reported a suicide rate in federal prisons from 1950 to 1969 of 10.5 per 100,000 per year — a rate that is actually lower than for the general population. He speculated that this low rate may be because federal prisoners have psychopathic traits that make *completed* suicides less likely (though we might expect manipulative suicide *attempts* to be more likely in such inmates). Schimmel and co-workers (1989) reported a suicide rate of 24 for federal prisons from 1983 to 1987.

Lester (1982, 1987a) calculated suicide rates for inmates in the whole of the United States for two time periods, 1978 to 1979 and 1980 to 1983. The rates for males were 24.6 and 24.3 respectively for these two time periods, 7.9 and 4.7 for women, 19.7 and 28.0 for federal male prisoners, and 25.2 and 24.0 for state male prisoners. These rates are about the same as the suicide rates for men in the general population in 1980 which was approximately 24.8 for men aged 25 to 34 years. Lester noted that these rates may be underestimates since in 1978-79, 8 percent of the deaths of federal prisoners and 19 percent of the deaths of state prisoners were listed as due to an unknown cause.

Burtch (1979a, 1979b) found the suicide rate in four maximum security prisons in Canada from 1959 to 1979 to be very high—272 per 100,000 per year. The suicide rate in Belgian prisons was reported to be 69, as compared to about 20 for men in the general population (Cosyns and Wilmotte 1974). Topp (1979) found that the suicide rate in English prisons had dropped between 1880 and 1971 from about 60 to about 40. There were peaks in the rate in 1916 and 1922 and a trough from 1937 to 1950. From 1958 to 1971, the suicide rate in English prisons was 42.

In the Netherlands, where all prison inmates have private cells, Kerkhof and Bernasco (1990) reported a prison suicide rate ranging from 62 per 100,000 per year to 207 for the years 1973 to 1985, whereas the national suicide rate for men aged 20 to 49 was in the range of 11.4 to 18.2 for these years. In Austria from 1957 to 1964, Hoff (1973) found a suicide rate of 81.

Thus, though some nations report higher suicide rates for men in prison than for men in the general population, the suicide rate of men in American prisons does not appear to be especially high. It is certainly less than in jails.

The Rate of Suicide: Death Row

Lester (1986) calculated a suicide rate of 146.5 for American prisoners on death row between 1977 and 1982. He commented that this was surprisingly high given the additional security typically imposed on prisoners on death row. This elevated figure may be due to the enormous stress of having to live with the fact that imposed death is imminent.

SUICIDE AMONG JUVENILES IN ADULT FACILITIES

In 1978, Flaherty (1980, 1983) examined the suicide rate of juveniles placed in adult detention facilities. The rates he reported were not right, so we have recalculated them, correcting them for the estimated length of stay of the juveniles in the different facilities. The suicide rates were 34 per 100,000 per year for juveniles in juvenile detention centers, 641 for juveniles in adult jails, and 1578 for juveniles in adult lockups. It can be seen that incarcerating juveniles in adult facilities is associated with a dramatic increase in the risk of suicide.

DISCUSSION

The first point of interest in these results is that the suicide rate in prisons appears to be stable. Lester (1982, 1987a) found a steady suicide rate nationally for U.S. prisoners over a five-year period. We can predict that from 20 to 30 prisoners out of every 100,000 will commit suicide each year. Thus, like the suicide rate of the society as a whole, the prison suicide rate is consistent and can be meaningfully studied.

Lester (1982) compared the suicide rates of male prisoners in each state with the suicide rates of men in the general population in each state. He found no association. Although the number of prison suicides in each state was small (making the suicide rates somewhat unreliable), his result suggests that the effects of prison are stronger than the effects of the region. (Suicide rates in general increase slightly toward the south in America and strongly toward the west.)

A second point is that, while the suicide rate in prisons is either average or a little above average, the suicide rate in jails is much higher than expected. This higher suicide rate among prisoners in jails may be because those prisoners are different in ways that are critical for determining the risk of suicide. Additionally, it may be that suicide prevention policies are less effective in jails than in prisons.

A third point of interest is the extremely high suicide rate reported for prisoners on death row. Because security procedures on death row are typically much tighter than for inmates in the general prison population, we would expect suicide to be less common on death row. The high suicide rate suggests that the stress of being under a sentence of death and on death row is so great that prisoners there make extraordinary efforts to kill themselves. Since those sentenced to death are socially isolated and heavily regulated, their suicides may be egoistic *and* fatalistic in nature.

A final point of interest is the high suicide rate of juveniles who are placed in adult facilities. This high rate suggests that it is much more stressful for juveniles to be placed in facilities for adults than it is for juveniles in facilities for juveniles. Lester's social deviancy theory is relevant here since it predicts that suicide should be more common in those who are sociologically deviant from the group of which they are a part; juvenile detainees do indeed show higher suicide rates when in adult prisons where they are sociologically deviant.

Chapter 3

Which Inmates Commit Suicide?

We have a good general idea of the kind of person who commits suicide in America. The typical suicide *completer* (those who are successful in killing themselves) is elderly, male, white, psychiatrically disturbed and lives alone. He tends to have a chronic history of stressful life events that may have increased in recent months and a history of suicidal behavior. In addition he uses a violent method for suicide such as a firearm. The typical suicide *attempter* (those who try to kill themselves, but do not succeed) in America is under 30 years of age, white, female and married. This individual tends to use an overdose of medications to attempt suicide.

It will be immediately apparent to readers in the field of corrections that prisoners who commit suicide do not fit into the above profiles; indeed inmates differ greatly from the typical non-inmate suicide. It is, therefore of great importance to identify the profile of the typical inmate suicide.

The question posed by the title of this chapter can be answered in two ways. There have been many reports, some based on very small samples of suicides, that describe the personal characteristics of the suicides in jail and prison. The results of studies based on small samples are not reliable and may not be typical to even that institution over a period of time and they are certainly not typical of other institutions. More importantly, the results of any reports are difficult to evaluate without knowing the characteristics of the typical *nonsuicidal* inmate in that particular institution. Therefore, more useful reports compare those who commit or attempt suicide in jail and prison with the nonsuicidal inmates to see which characteristics are more common in the suicidal inmates. In this chapter we will briefly review both types of reports.

THE TYPICAL SUICIDAL INMATE

Police Lockups

Danto (1989) presented a profile of a typical kind of suicide that occurs in police lockups. Typically the suicide occurs soon after booking, usually within the first three hours. The suicidal person is a white male under the age of 22, arrested for a relatively nonserious and nonviolent crime. He is often intoxicated and is belligerent, confrontational and assaultive toward the investigating officers. Most often the suicide is committed by hanging — using a shirt, shoelaces, underwear or socks — after the inmate is placed in an isolation cell that is poorly supervised. He does not have a chronic history of criminal behavior and is basically law-abiding. He often feels impotent and angry because he was not able to avoid arrest, and he feels embarrassed, especially over the impact his arrest will have on his family. Thus, his plight becomes invested with more meaning than it deserves.

Niemi (1978) reported that hanging was the most common method for suicide among inmates in lockups in Finland. He found no variation in the suicide rate by day of the week or by month.

Jails

Danto (1989) described the typical jail suicide as a male who has committed a serious or violent crime, such as murder, rape, felonious assault, assault and battery or breaking and entering. He will hang himself, usually at night between the hours of 11:00 p.m. and 6:00 a.m. when there is less supervision. The suicide occurs either a few days after incarceration or a few months later as the trial approaches and/or after sentencing has been completed. He will be in his thirties, with a poor marital and employment history, an unstable life style, and a history of psychiatric problems. In the east and in the midwest the suicidal inmate is African American and in the west he is Hispanic. Cases involving native Americans are common in the southwest.

Danto (1972) described ten suicides that took place in the Wayne County jail in Detroit. The typical suicide was a black male who was charged with a violent crime and whose suicide occurred after about two to four weeks of incarceration. Seven of the inmates had either no prospect of being released on bail or else bail had been set so high that they had no chance of paying it; in other words these seven men knew that there was no chance of leaving jail in the near future. Danto noted that several of the ten men had been moved frequently within the jail on the orders of the deputy sheriffs who thought that this helped depressed or agitated inmates, though such a tactic is probably not a good idea.

Smialek and Spitz (1978) also described 22 suicides in the Wayne County jail and found that the majority were white males who hanged themselves. Alcohol or drugs were found during the post-mortem examination in 9 of the 20 suicides. Eight had been booked on minor charges. Almost all of the suicides occurred within the first 24 hours of incarceration. Also studying the Wayne County jail, Burtka and associates (1988) found the typical suicide to be male and to have died by hanging in a single cell within in the first three weeks of incarceration and during the 11:00 p.m. to 7:00 a.m. shift.

One-third of those who committed suicide were charged with actual or attempted murder or manslaughter.

Heilig (1973) found the typical suicide in the Los Angeles County jails to be a white male in his twenties, who was charged with being intoxicated with drugs or alcohol, and who died by hanging within the first 24 hours of incarceration.

Esparza (1973) found the typical suicide in six midwestern jails to be a single, white male with a mean age of 29, a record of violent crimes and a history of prior suicide attempts and psychiatric contacts, who died by hanging within the first 12 weeks of incarceration.

Frost and Hanzlick (1988) identified 14 suicides in the Atlanta and Fulton County jails over an 11-year period. All chose hanging, using belts, clothing or bed linens. They found that the majority of the victims had committed crimes against persons and other serious offenses.

Tracy (1972) reported on the suicides in the New York City jails between 1970 and 1971. The average age of the victims was 23 years and the average period of incarceration was 14 days. Many were Puerto Ricans, all were males, and all of them hanged themselves. Suicide was more common in the morning that in the afternoon, and almost half of the suicides were narcotic addicts. Novick and Remmlinger (1978) found that the typical suicide in New York City correctional facilities was between the ages of 35 and 44 (mean age 29), a detainee awaiting trial for a violent crime, with a history of substance abuse and psychiatric problems, held in the mental observation area, who died by hanging within the first two weeks of incarceration.

Jordan and co-workers (1987) identified 17 suicides in Oklahoma jails from 1981 to 1983. Sixteen of these employed hanging, and the typical suicide was a single white male, 25 to 34 years of age (mean age 29), arrested for an alcohol-related crime, and with a blood ethanol level greater than 0.10 mg/dl. Half of the suicides occurred within 12 hours of incarceration and 88 percent within 48 hours. More suicides took place in autumn, and on Wednesdays at about 6:00 a.m.

Kennedy (1984) described the typical suicide in local lockups and county jails in Michigan in 1980 and 1981 as white,

25 to 29 years of age, in a lockup rather than a county jail, charged with a more serious offense, and dying within 12 hours of incarceration.

Stone (1990) examined 107 suicides in Texas jails between 1986 and 1988. Of these, 66 occurred in county jails and 41 in municipal jails. The typical suicide was white, aged 23 to 25 years and died by hanging.

Hankoff (1980) examined seven inmate suicides in one eastern city, all of whom were male, and whose deaths occurred by hanging in the late night hours. Their average age was 28 years. None left suicide notes. Four had communicated suicidal ideation prior to their deaths, and four were diagnosed as psychiatrically disturbed while incarcerated. Hankoff concluded that five of the seven were both psychiatrically disturbed and substance abusers and committed suicide at a time when they were acutely disturbed (confused and disoriented).

Copeland (1984, 1989) described 23 suicides in correctional facilities in Dade County, Florida. The typical suicide was a white male, in his twenties, who had a psychiatric disorder—most commonly schizophrenia. All 23 employed hanging. The most common offense was armed robbery. Thirteen percent had significant levels of alcohol in their blood, and six cases tested positive for drugs. Of those, only one of these had taken cocaine and one had taken methaqualone. The suicides happened most often within the first 24 hours of arrest, between midnight and noon.

Lanphear (1987) identified eight suicides over a 15-year period in a county detention center in Tennessee. The typical suicide was male. Even though he tested positive for alcohol, he could not be considered legally intoxicated. Half of the suicides were white and half were black. All of them died by hanging. Their ages ranged from 21 to 39, with a mean age of 33.

In Cuyahoga County (Cleveland) from 1956 to 1967, there were 23 suicides (Adelson et al. 1968). The typical suicide was a white male, aged 31 to 40, who died by hanging. The most common means for hanging were belts (13), neckties (2), shirt sleeves (2), towels (2), a pant leg (1), a coat lining (1), and a sling for an injured arm (1). Eighty-three percent of the suicides occurred within the first 24 hours of incarceration, and 61 percent within 6 hours. Seventy-four percent had some alcohol detected in their blood, and this percentage was similar for those charged with alcohol and non-alcohol-related offenses. Seventy-percent of the suicides took place within 30 minutes of being seen alive by a guard. None of the prisoners had voiced any suicidal messages to the guards. Two of the prisoners had been examined by physicians after arrest, but suicidal tendencies were not detected.

Hayes (1983) surveyed all county and local jails in the United States during 1979 and discovered 419 suicides. The typical suicide was a single white male, 22 years old, arrested for public intoxication, with no history of prior arrests, placed in isolation for his own protection or for surveillance, and dead within 3 hours by hanging. The most common time for the suicide was between midnight and 1:00 a.m. on a Saturday night in September.

Hayes (1989; Hayes and Rowan 1988) reported a national study of jail suicides in 1985-86 that identified a similar profile: a single white male, aged 23 to 27, who was intoxicated. He had no prior charges, was a detainee held in isolation on a nonviolent charge, not screened for suicidal risk, who committed suicide by hanging (using bedding) within the first 24 hours of incarceration between midnight and 3:00 a.m.

Prisons

Anno (1985) found that the typical suicide among the sentenced offenders in the Texas Department of Corrections was a single, white, Catholic male under 30 years of age (mean age 30), with one or more prior arrests, who was sentenced for a crime against a person (as opposed to property crimes, though burglary/theft was the single most common offense). Those with prison sentences of less than five years and more than 25 years accounted for about one-third of the inmate suicides. The most common interval between incarceration and suicide occurred after inmates served one to two years. Eighty-nine percent of the men committed suicide by hanging, two slashed their necks, one jumped from a water tower and one overdosed on barbiturates.

In the Maryland state prison system, Salive and associates (1989) found that the typical suicide among prisoners with sentences of one year or more was black, aged 25 to 34 (mean age 29), sentenced for crimes against persons (murder being the most common crime), in a maximum security institution, with a sentence longer than 97 months, after serving an average of 43 months in prison, with death by hanging. (There was no variation by month or day of the week.)

Schimmel and co-workers (1989) described the typical suicide in the federal prison system from 1983 to 1987 as a hanging, in a single-occupancy cell (no suicides occurred among inmates who had cellmates or were on suicide watch), between midnight 5:00 a.m. in May or June. One-third of the victims were psychotic and 44 percent had made prior suicide attempts at some point in their lives.

In an Australian prison that held both sentenced prisoners and offenders awaiting trial, the most common method was hanging and the mean age of the suicides was 24. Richert (1974) reported that the typical suicide in French prisons in 1972 was a male, 20 to 29 years of age, in preventive detention (i.e., awaiting trial), dying in the second half of the month, with a peak in October. There was no excess of prison suicides on major national holidays. Suicide seemed to be more common among those of North African nationality (especially Algerians and Moroccans), less common among those of Spanish and Portuguese descent, and least common among the French. In Belgian penitentiaries, Cosyns and Wilmotte (1974) found that indicted inmates were more suicidal in the first three days of incarceration than were convicted inmates.

In Canadian maximum security prisons, between the years 1959 and 1975, Burtch (1979a, 1979b) found the typical suicide to have killed himself by hanging, during the early stages of incarceration. He was unmarried, serving a sentence either as short as two to three years or the total opposite—life. A large number of the victims had previously received psychiatric treatment and had made prior attempts at suicide. There was no predominance of crimes against people over crimes against property and no variation in hours of the day or month.

In an English prison, between the years 1958 and 1971, Topp (1979) found the typical suicide to be unmarried, sentenced (rather than awaiting trial), 25 to 34 years of age, charged with or convicted of theft, with prior convictions and incarcerations, and serving the first month of imprisonment. The peak day that suicides occurred was Saturday and the peak time was during the night. The most common method was hanging, and almost two-thirds of the inmates had been seen by the medical/psychiatric staff while in custody. Topp postulated that those who committed suicide were perhaps acting impulsively, were seeking attention, and that maybe they expected to be saved.

Backett (1987) found the typical suicide in Scottish prisons from the year 1970 to 1982, to be a single male with prior convictions, awaiting trial or sentencing, in the first month of imprisonment. The average age was 29. A significant number of the victims had a history of prior suicide attempts and psychiatric treatment. Interestingly, a third were under observation at the time that they killed themselves, and four of the 33 victims were being watched as suicide risks.

In Dutch prisons, from 1964 to 1985, Kerkhof (1987) found that suicide was most common early in the incarceration, that hanging was the most common method for suicide and more than half of the deaths occurred during the first three months. There was no variation over particular months and days. More than half of the victims had visited the prison physician in the week prior to their deaths, and 20 percent communicated their suicidal preoccupation to this doctor.

Discussion

The only correctional facility for which a large number of suicide reports have appeared is jails. All of these reports agree that the typical inmate suicide is male, and most agree that he is in his twenties and dies by hanging. There is less agreement on whether he has the following characteristics: unmarried, intoxicated, an addict, psychiatrically disturbed, committing suicide in the morning, on Wednesdays, in the autumn, and in the first few days of incarceration. Many of the studies find that the typical case is white, but occasional studies find that he is black or Puerto Rican. The studies are divided on whether the crime that caused incarceration is a serious one against people or a minor crime, and whether it is alcohol-related.

It is clear that the samples Hayes used are quite small, but there is obvious merit in his studies on national samples (1988, 1989). Because the profile of the typical inmate suicide may differ in each community, there also is merit in local studies that, necessarily, are based on smaller samples. There are far fewer studies of the inmates of prisons, and it is clear that more research is needed on these institutions.

COMPARISONS

Jails and Lockups

Frost and Hanzlick (1988) found that prisoners who committed suicide in jail were more likely to have committed crimes against persons than those dying from other causes (62 percent versus 38 percent). Copeland (1984) compared the prisoners who committed suicide in Dade County (Miami) with those dying of other causes. The suicides were more likely to be male and younger (in their twenties), but did not differ in race.

In Michigan lockups and county jails, Kennedy (1984) found that the suicides tended to be charged with more serious crimes, but they did not differ from the general prisoners in race or age. In a later study of the Wayne County jail, the suicides again did not differ from other inmates in race or age (Burtka et al. 1988).

Prisons

Anno (1985) looked at suicide in sentenced offenders in the Texas Department of Corrections from 1980 to 1985. He found that the suicides were similar to other inmates in age and sex. The suicides differed from other inmates in that they were more likely to be white or Hispanic, were more often single or divorced, more often Catholic, and tended to have one or more prior arrests. Murderers were more likely to commit suicide than other offenders, and Anno suggested (he presented no data) that those who murdered their own family members were especially likely to commit suicide.

In the federal prison system from 1983 to 1987, Schimmel and co-workers (1989) found an overrepresentation of Hispanics and especially of Cuban detainees from the Mariel exodus in 1980. Suicide was more common in pre-sentenced inmates and in those with long sentences (20 years or more). The Cuban Mariel suicides were primarily men held in solitary confinement (because of antisocial behavior), who were diagnosed as having an antisocial or borderline personality disorder.

In Canadian prisons, Burtch (1979a, 1979b) found that those who committed suicide were less likely to be married than other inmates, were more often in their teens or twenties or over 50, were more likely to be charged with a violent crime, and were more likely to be in punitive detention, protective custody or the prison hospital.

In reviewing the literature, Haycock (1991a), admitted that the suicide rate in prisons was much lower than in jails, but he felt that certain groups of prisoners were at higher risk of suicide; men convicted of murder, those serving life sentences or under sentence of death, and those in maximum security institutions. Contrary to expectations, Haycock claims that the suicide risk does not appear to be higher early in the sentence or prior to release. (Haycock claims that research studies document his conclusions, but many of the studies he cited are unpublished and, therefore, hard to locate.)

Haycock pointed out that the prison population in America is aging. Prisoners over the age of 55 are the fastest-growing demographic group in prisons, and these men have typically committed more serious offenses and have received longer sentences. Since suicide rates in general rise with age in America, Haycock warned that the suicide rate might well grow over time. Furthermore, the increasing prevalence of AIDS among inmates also leads to a prediction of higher prison suicide rates in the future.

Race and Suicide

Anson and Cole (1984) noted that the suicides in the Florida Department of Corrections were more often white than they would have expected. Anson (1983) noted that prison suicide rates were higher in those states where there were higher proportions of white inmates and lower proportions of black inmates (but this was not associated with the proportions of native American, Asian or Hispanic inmates). Anson and Cole argued that blacks (who have a relatively low suicide rate in prison) have stronger peer group relations while incarcerated than do whites, while Hispanics (who have a high suicide rate in prison) suffer more from the loss of family support while in prison. However, Anson's argument is weakened by the fact that these ethnic differences in suicide rates exist in the general population as well.

It is interesting to note that in recent years in Australia there has been a good deal of concern over the high rate at which aborigines are committing suicide in custody. The typical aborigine suicide fits the profile of the typical suicide in American local jails — young, male, charged with a minor offense and intoxicated (Hunter 1988). Australian commentators have focused on the intoxication factor and the removal of the individual from his home territory to a distant prison, stressing that the bond between the Australian aborigine and the place in which he lives is very strong (Spencer 1989). Incarceration may lead to feelings of anomie, helplessness, powerlessness and depression.

Discussion

Clearly, there are far fewer studies comparing suicidal inmates with nonsuicidal inmates than there are studies that simply describe a sample of inmate suicides. Yet these comparison studies are critical for devising simple checklists to help identify which inmates should be considered potential suicides. We need to know how suicidal inmates differ from nonsuicidal inmates, and not simply by utilizing the obvious characteristics of sex, race, marital status and age, but also other easily obtained information, such as prior arrest record, education, religion and religious behavior, sibling position and family size, and childhood experiences (such as physical punishment and physical abuse, parental loss through death or divorce, and illnesses and injuries), to name a few.

IS THERE A SUICIDAL PROFILE?

Part of the usefulness of identifying which demographic and psychological characteristics are more commonly found in suicidal prisoners is that we may be able to identify a suicide-prone personality and thereby identify the potential suicide before he kills himself.

The inconsistencies in the findings reviewed above have led some researchers, such as Kennedy (1984), to view this task as useless, but we will examine this issue in detail in Chapter 6 and will show that meaningful profiles can be very useful.

Suicidal Types

Despite reservations, some writers have identified commonly occurring types among suicidal inmates, and though these typologies have not been studied for their reliability (or generalizability) or their usefulness, it is worthwhile information, especially for to those working in correctional facilities. Danto (1971) has described the following types:

Morality Shock. This individual becomes suicidal shortly after admission when he has to come to terms with his criminal behavior and its consequences—the disgrace and embarrassment he has brought to himself and to his family. He usually does not have a significant criminal history, and his life has been stable and law-abiding in work and marriage. His crime might be violent (first- or second-degree murder), a publicized sexual offense or a white-collar crime such as embezzlement. The person, though typically a moral individual, has let his guard down and behaved in such a way as to grossly offend even his own moral code.

Chronic Despair. This inmate has been in the post-sentence detention center for several months following sentencing. He has developed a persistent sense of hopelessness and futility about his future. He feels disconnected from his family, friends and even his attorney. Signs of humanness, like a name, have been replaced by prison symbols, like a number. He often has a history of previous incarcerations in which he felt similarly hopeless and isolated. Suicide is for him an escape from this despair. It is not unusual for the staff to *unconsciously* concur with his decision, believing that his suicide will not only help the inmate, but also will rid the society of a hardened criminal.

Manipulative. The antisocial individual who seeks to manipulate others to satisfy his own desires may make nonlethal suicide attempts in order to manipulate the guards and prison administrators. He may view transfer to the prison hospital as a softer assignment. Or he may simply seek preferential treatment because of his suicidal state. He typically cuts his wrists or swallows glass. Although this type of person can be goaded into suicide by those around him, a lethal outcome is rare since he is using suicidal behavior to enhance his life, not to end it.

Self-Punishment. A different type of suicide attempter mutilates himself in order to humiliate himself and to make life as painful and as miserable as possible. Indeed, his criminal behavior may also be a part of this pattern of self-punishment.

He feels guilty about sexual desires and other behaviors that
he views as sinful. These inmates have often been violent
toward themselves and others in the past.

FINAL COMMENT

Although the research reported in this chapter may be quite
limited in its usefulness, it does suggest the kind of study that
needs to be done in the future, using larger samples and a
greater variety of inmate characteristics. Furthermore, despite
the speculative nature of Danto's typology, it is obvious that
not all suicidal inmates are alike and that typologies will be
meaningful and more useful than a single overall profile.

Chapter 4

Suicide Attempts and Self-Mutilation

It is estimated in America that for every one person who *completes* a suicide (i.e, dies) eight or more people *attempt* to kill themselves (i.e., survive). This same ratio seems to hold true for inmates of prisons and jails (see, for example, Esparza 1973). Suicide attempters often make relatively nonlethal gestures at suicide, such as taking a handful of aspirin or making light cuts across their wrists. Many do not require any medical treatment and do not come to the attention of the authorities. Other suicide attempters, however, do make a serious effort to kill themselves and are saved through the chance intervention of others or because the would-be suicide made errors in his attempt (such as miscalculating the lethal overdose).

In America, the typical completed suicide in the general population is an elderly white male, while the typical suicide attempter is a young female. Thus, it is often argued by scholars that completed suicides and attempted suicides have little or nothing in common. It is also believed by many that those who attempt suicide are not especially high suicide risks. For a number of reasons both of these beliefs are false.

First of all, the risk of completed suicide is very high in those who attempt suicide. Whereas about 1.4 percent of

Americans die from suicide (see Chapter 2), almost 15 percent of attempted suicides ultimately die from suicide (Lester 1989a). Thus, previously attempting suicide is a sign of high suicide risk, as we shall see in Chapter 6.

Second, it is not true that completed suicides and attempted suicides have almost nothing in common. For example, Lester and associates (1979) took a sample people who had attempted suicide and asked them whether they really intended to kill themselves. Some said "no," some were "not sure," and others said "yes." Lester found that the average level of depression, as measured by a self-report questionnaire, was low for those who did not intend to die, higher for those who were uncertain and highest for those who intended to die. Thus, depression scores increased monotonically from mild to serious suicide attempts, and so we could predict that completed suicides (the most serious of all) would have even higher depression scores. Several years later, a number of these original suicide attempters did kill themselves, and these were the most depressed when tested originally, years earlier. Lester concluded that attempted suicides and completed suicides do share common traits and that it is possible to learn about completed suicides from the study of attempted suicides. (Lester also classified the suicide attempters into three groups on the basis of objective actions taken during the suicide attempt, such as taking care to isolate oneself in order to prevent intervention by others; he obtained the same results.)

Furthermore, since there are about eight to ten suicide attempts for every completed suicide, the 300,000 attempted suicides that occur yearly in the United States create a fair amount of work for medical facilities. Some suicide attempters make repeated attempts at suicide (Lester 1987b). These repeaters can be a burden for health care facilities; health care workers, such as emergency room staff, are often quite hostile toward suicide attempters; they resent what they consider to be time "wasted" on the care of these patients while medically sick people await attention (Dressler et al. 1975).

We would argue that, since a suicide attempt is a predictor of a high risk for a future completed suicide, correctional staff should view suicide attempts as *useful* for their evaluation of the inmate's suicidal potential. Questioning the inmate carefully and sensitively regarding his thoughts about his suicide attempt and his reasons for doing it provides useful information that can be instrumental in preventing his possible successful suicide.

HOW COMMON IS ATTEMPTED SUICIDE IN PRISONS?

Sloane (1973) identified all of the attempted suicides that took place from 1970 to 1972 in Washington, D.C. correctional institutions. The rate of attempted suicides in jails was 3200 per 100,000 inmates per year and the rate of attempted suicide in prisons was 1380.

Payson (1975), who worked in two small state prisons, estimated that about 15 percent of the inmates expressed verbal threats or made overt suicidal gestures during their stays, particularly during the initial period or incarceration.

Albanese (1983) studied pretrial and short-sentence offenders in a federal correctional institution. Their average stay was 26 days. In 18 months there were 44 suicide attempts and one completed suicide, and these constituted 13 percent of the injuries that required treatment in the institution during that period. The one completed suicide victim made several attempts prior to his death, the first one of which was merely a superficial cut. This example supports what we have said — that even mild suicidal gestures can be indicative of increased suicidal risk and eventual completed suicide.

In Belgium, Wilmotte and Plat-Mendlewicz (1973) found that 2.4 percent of juvenile delinquents attempted suicide while awaiting trial. In Austrian prisons from 1957 to 1964, Hoff (1973) found the rate of attempted suicide to be 378 per 100,000 per year.

Attempted Suicide Before Incarceration

In a survey of federal prisoners in one institution, Rieger (1971) found that 7 percent of the inmates had attempted suicide at some point during their lives. Lester (1991a) found that 20 percent of the inmates in the Vermont prison system had previously attempted suicide. In Australia, Koller and Castanos (1969) found that 12 percent of sentenced male prisoners (both short-term and long-term) and 36 percent of short-term female prisoners had attempted suicide at some point in their lives. In Belgium, Wilmotte and Plat-Mendelwicz (1973) found that 6 percent of juvenile delinquents awaiting trial had attempted suicide before they came to the attention of the law.

STUDIES OF SUICIDE ATTEMPTERS

Prior Suicide Attempts

Rieger (1971) studied 58 inmates who had previously attempted suicide in one federal prison. (He does not report where the previous suicide attempts took place.) The typical attempter was male, white, slightly more likely to have committed a violent crime than a property crime, and equally likely to be Roman Catholic or "Other." The typical attempt was mild (1 on a scale of 1 to 4), and the most common method was wrist-cutting. The experience of a recent loss was rare.

Compared to the rest of the prison population, the suicide attempters did not differ in race, religion or in the crime they committed. The more serious suicide attempts were made by inmates who had suffered a recent loss (within the last six months), who used methods other than cutting, and who had made previous attempts at suicide. The more serious attempters were *less* likely to have been separated from their mothers at an early age.

In the Vermont prison system, Lester (1991a) found that

inmates who had previously attempted suicide had committed more serious and assaultive crimes and were more assaultive while in prison. They had been physically abused more often by their parents and physically punished more often by their fathers. They had received more prior psychiatric treatment, had less stable living arrangements, less often had a history of being self-supporting, had less satisfying interpersonal relationships, had less appropriate responses to anger and to depression, had more pessimism about the future, more back and stomach problems, more serious head injuries, less education, and more often had parents who abused alcohol.

Griffiths (1990) compared English male inmates who had attempted suicide at some point in their lives with inmates who had not. The suicide attempters more often had family members with a psychiatric disturbance and a criminal record. Their families were full of discord and disruptions of all kinds (including parental loss and parental fighting). The suicide attempters more often had no friends as children, and they disliked school more. They more often had broken marriages, psychiatric disturbance and prior convictions, and they more often abused drugs and alcohol.

In Canada, Dyck and co-workers (1990) found a lifetime incidence of attempted suicide of 23 percent in male inmates aged 18 to 44. The suicide attempters were more often diagnosed as having a substance abuse disorder, an antisocial personality disorder, an affective disorder and anxiety and somatoform disorders. They were also more depressed and suicidal in prison, but they did not differ in the history of violent behavior.

Wilmotte and Plat-Mendelwicz (1973) found that young men in Belgium awaiting trial, who had attempted suicide at some point in their lives, were more often foreigners (especially French), more often divorced or separated and, if married they were without children, less often the first-born, used cutting, and their attempts were mostly precipitated by marital problems. The highest incidence of suicide attempts was in those charged with drug offenses, theft with violence, and forgery (17 to 22 percent) and lowest for those charged with fraud, outrage on decency and theft (6 to 7 percent).

Suicide Attempts in Jail and Prison

In a federal institution for pretrial offenders and short- sentence prisoners, Albanese (1983) found that most of the suicide attempts were made by cutting, during the first 24 hours of incarceration, between 10:00 p.m. and 1:00 a.m. Twenty percent of the suicide attempters had scars on their wrists or arms on admission. Compared to the other prisoners, the suicide attempters were more often white and single, less often Protestant and more often had made threats on the President's life or threatened to destroy government property. They did not differ in sex, age or education from other prisoners.

Sloane (1973) compared jail and prison inmates who attempted suicide while incarcerated with those who did not. In jail, the attempted suicides were younger than the non-attempters, had committed more serious offenses, were more often disciplinary problems, and were less often addicted to drugs. In prison, the attempters were a little younger than the non-attempters, had shorter sentences and had been incarcerated for a shorter period of time. The lethality of the suicide attempt was associated with the seriousness of the crime for jail inmates and with a history of previous suicide attempts for prison inmates.

In six midwestern jails, Esparza (1973) found those who attempted suicide while in jail to be single and white, with a mean age of 24 (younger than the completed suicides), using cutting and making attempts of low lethality, in the first three weeks of incarceration and between 4:00 p.m. and midnight.

DeHeer and Schweitzer (1985) compared prisoners who made suicide attempts in the county jail in Eugene, Oregon with those put on suicidal watch but who did not make a suicide attempt. The two groups had a similar profile — white, male, on drugs or alcohol when admitted, and usually at highest risk in the first 24 hours of incarceration. The majority of the suicide attempters (65 percent) had made attempts of minimum lethality, used hanging, had a history of attempting suicide, and were in prison for minor offenses.

Hopes and Shaull (1986) studied eleven suicide attempters at the county jail in Cincinnati. Ten of them had been referred for a psychiatric evaluation upon admission. (Of the 2000 new inmates in a five-month period, 161 had been sent for a psychiatric evaluation.) Ten of the eleven attempted suicide in the first week or in the week prior to trial or sentencing. They were mainly felons awaiting transfer to a state prison. Those who attempted suicide were often substance abusers, had suicidal ideation, felt hopeless and had attempted suicide five or more times in the past.

In the New York City correctional system, Gaston (1979) examined 85 completed suicides and 224 attempted suicides. He described the typical suicidal inmate as male, Hispanic or Catholic, aged 21 to 25, with an education of 6th through 9th grade, married, with sporadic employment, who was not an addict. He had reactive (rather than endogenous) depression, had made prior suicide attempts, felt anger and experienced hallucinations, had committed property crimes, and used hanging, in the summer, between midnight and 8:00 a.m., in the first three days of incarceration, or after 60 days. It would have been more helpful, of course, if Gaston had differentiated between those who had completed and those who had attempted suicide.

Haycock (1989b) compared inmates who had made lethal attempts at suicide with those who made nonlethal attempts, all of whom had been sent to a state psychiatric hospital for evaluation and treatment. The attempters who used more lethal methods were older, more often the first-born or only children, more often were drunk at the time of the suicidal act, and more often were heroin users, with more prior suicide attempts, recent family turmoil, depression, hopelessness and inward-directed hostility. (The attempters did not differ from the completers in marital status, unemployment, religious affiliation, parental loss in childhood, type of charge, bail status, prior incarceration, alcohol abuse, prior psychiatric care, psychiatric diagnosis, or family support while incarcerated.) It is significant that the important differences identified by Haycock were the same as those found by researchers who studied non-inmate suicide attempters. The offense and prison experience were not differentiated between the groups.

Power and Spencer (1987) looked at juvenile Scottish prisoners aged 16 to 21, who had attempted or threatened suicide. Forty-nine percent had threatened suicide, 31 percent lacerated their wrist or arm, 8 percent set fire to their cell furnishings, 7 percent swallowed items, and 5 percent feigned hanging. The majority of the suicide attempts were of low lethality: 92 percent were of minimal lethality, 4 percent were of moderate lethality, and 4 percent were of high lethality.

Half of these inmates stated that their suicidal behavior was instigated because they were seeking protection from anticipated friction with fellow inmates. Another quarter simply wanted to be transferred to what they considered more convivial surroundings. However, 18 percent had experienced a recent stressful event, such as sentencing or rejection by a girlfriend. Three percent were judged to be psychiatrically disturbed.

Beigel and Russell (1972) found that inmates who attempted suicide in Arizona jails were younger than other inmates (23 versus 29 years of age), were more often separated and divorced, were less likely to have committed violent crimes, were more often recidivists, and were more likely to have attempted suicide before being sent to jail. Suicide attempts were more common in the first six weeks of incarceration.

In prisons in the Netherlands, Kerkhof and Bernasco (1990) found that inmates who attempted suicide primarily used cutting (whereas the completed suicides died by hanging), acted impulsively, had been showing suicidal ideation for some time and had communicated this to others. About a third alerted the staff to their actions after making their suicide attempt. Although attempts were common throughout the entire period of incarceration, a slight majority occurred in the first month. There was no variation over the days of the week. The attempts occurred most often between 10:00 p.m. and 6:00 a.m. (whereas the completed suicides showed no variation over the hours of the day). The attempters were often substance abusers who had attempted suicide in the past. They were more often under stress from relatives, the legal process, their substance abuse and prison life. The attempted suicides were younger then nonsuicidal inmates, were less often employed, were more often Muslim and less often Dutch, were more often charged with murder or manslaughter, were serving longer sentences, were more often on medication, and had frequently visited the prison physician in the week prior to the suicide attempt.

Wool and Dooley (1987) found an attempted suicide rate in one English prison of 817 (per 100,000 per year). The typical suicide attempter was in a local prison, was aged 19 to 21 years old, awaiting trial, and had suffered recent domestic stress (such as not having a visitor or receiving bad news from home). Domestic stress was the most common precipitant (43 percent), prison stress was next (25 percent), followed by fear/guilt/anger (16 percent) and psychosis (5 percent).

It is worth noting that cutting is not always the most commonly reported method for attempted suicide. Two studies from Italy report hanging as the most common method for attempted suicide in one prison (Pittalis et al. 1990) and starvation in another (De Fazio and Gualandri 1990).

Attempted Suicide in Female Prisoners

Lorettu and associates (1990) discussed the influence of female homosexuality in prison on the occurrence of attempted suicide. They documented that more suicide attempts occurred after a woman experienced separation from her homosexual lover.

SINGLE VERSUS MULTIPLE ATTEMPTERS

Le Brun (1989) compared inmates a made a single attempt with those who made several attempts during incarceration at the Sacramento County jail. The majority of both groups had made threats about committing suicide and had made actual suicide attempts in the past, were psychiatrically disturbed, had experienced hallucinations or delusions and had prior psychiatric contacts and arrests.

The single attempters tended to make more attempts on weekdays, close to court dates, during the first two months of incarceration, while the multiple attempters tried suicide close to meaningful anniversaries, on weekends, that were usually precipitated by relationship problems and during the first few weeks of incarceration. The single attempters were more often psychotic, whereas the multiple attempters more often had personality disorders. The single attempters made more lethal attempts and their prior arrests were more often for violent crimes against people, whereas the multiple attempters had a record of alcohol/drug and minor offenses.

SUICIDE ATTEMPTERS VERSUS COMPLETERS

Fawcett and Marrs (1973) compared a sample of completed suicides in the Cook County jail with a sample of suicide attempters judged to have high suicidal intent. The two groups were similar in racial makeup (there was an overrepresentation of whites, Puerto Ricans and Mexicans), charge (violent crimes were most common), timing (early in incarceration), precipitants (rejection by significant others), and psychiatric background (a high incidence of prior suicide attempts and psychiatric disturbance). Interestingly, both groups used hanging most often as the method of suicide. The attempters were younger than the completers.

Based on his experience in the New York City correctional system, Gaston (1979) described the typical suicide attempter as nonaggressive. His criminal acts allow him to "escape" and avoid confrontation and are mainly property crimes. His suicide attempt in prison is an attempt to escape from confrontations he cannot face.

The typical suicide completer in prison is an aggressor. He commits crimes of violence and he overpowers his victims so he can feel like he is in control. In prison he loses this control and perhaps kills himself to prove that he still exercises ultimate control over his fate.

TYPES OF SUICIDE ATTEMPTS

Sloane (1973) felt that suicidal attempts made by prisoners could be classified into three types. *Depressive* suicide attempts are most common during the initial days of incarceration and result from the depressed mood and hopelessness felt by prisoners who have been charged with a crime and are awaiting trial or who have recently been sentenced. *Manipulative* suicide attempts are committed for the anticipated gain expected as a result. The risk of such attempts is probably constant during the period of incarceration. *Anomic* suicide attempts increase with frequency during the period of incarceration and result from the impact of the long imprisonment on the inmate's feelings of alienation, powerlessness and helplessness.

SUICIDAL IDEATION

Jones (1976) found that 32 percent of the white inmates and 3 percent of the black prisoners in a Tennessee prison had thoughts of suicide. Suicidal ideation was more common in the younger inmates (younger than 25), those who were married and those who were less educated.

In a Florida county jail, Bonner and Rich (1989) found that 77 percent of the inmates had some suicidal ideation; 28 percent had mild thoughts, 20 percent moderate and 29 percent high.

SELF-MUTILATION IN PRISON

Prisoners often mutilate themselves without having any suicidal intent. This behavior is called *self-mutilation* or *self-in-*

jurious behavior. The most common forms of self-mutilation in the general population are head-banging, eye-gouging, biting fingers and other parts of the body, scratching and rectal poking. In correctional settings the most common forms of self-mutilation are laceration of the body with razor blades or other sharp objects and ingestion of foreign objects such as metal utensils or razor blades (Martinez 1980). This behavior can be repetitive. Martinez reported one prisoner who repeatedly ingested foreign objects resulting in more than 60 operations over a period of several years at a tremendous cost for medical care.

People who mutilate themselves, especially by cutting, often remark that they feel numb or empty before committing the act. The pain and the sight of blood restore their feelings of identity. These triggering feelings of depersonalization and lack of identity are, of course, made worse by the routine and lack of individuality caused by being in an institution.

Cookson (1977) noted that self-mutilation by inmates can have several causes. It can be a way of punishing themselves for real or imagined sins and feeling of unworthiness. Self-mutilation often seems to relieve feelings of depression and tenseness and gives the individual a sense of personal control. Self-mutilators may also be identifying with their aggressors. In other words, they are acting toward themselves in the same way the custodial staff acts toward them. Self-mutilation can also be a source of stimulation for a person who is suffering from sensory deprivation and boredom.

Wicks (1974) has suggested several other reasons for self-mutilation:

1. *Reclassification*: The inmate may want a transfer to another part of the prison either out of concern for his personal safety, to give himself some control over his fate, or to be with friends who are in other units.

2. *Cry for help*: The inmate may want to attract attention to be given to himself, such as better services (medication or food), or help in dealing with the institutional staff who have ignored or aggravated his problems.

3. *Escape from intolerable situations*: The inmate may wish to escape from the prison environment, from depression, or from guilt over his crime.

4. *Desire for clemency*: The inmate may hope that a record of self-mutilation may convince judges, parole boards and staff to treat him more kindly and with greater consideration.

Ross and co-workers (1978) classified the reasons for self-mutilation as personal (such as for relieving tension, relaxing, or proving that one is alive) and prison-oriented (such as protection against ill-treatment, escape from brutality, an attempt to receive therapeutic intervention, and manipulating staff for secondary gain).

Characteristics of Self-Mutilators

Beto and Claghorn (1968) compared mentally disturbed felons in Texas who self-mutilated with felons who did not. The self-mutilators were more likely to be Hispanic (and, if Hispanic, drug addicts), to come from larger families and to have poorer occupational adjustment (i.e., to be migrant workers, drifters, or professional criminals). The two groups did not differ in age, duration of psychiatric treatment, criminal offense, marital status, military history, sexual adjustment, or time served in prison.

In North Carolina prisons, Johnson (1973) found that inmates who engaged in self-mutilation were more often unmarried whites, had fewer prior convictions (perhaps because they were younger), and who more often rule violators and attempted escapees than the other inmates. The self-mutilators primarily used cutting and were typically in special holding facilities when they committed this act. The two most common reasons were manipulation of correctional staff and general anxiety.

At a home for delinquent girls in Canada, Ross and co-workers (1978) described a self-mutilating behavior that was common in that institution; the girls carved specific symbols into their skin. Names were most common, followed by initials and words. Those who carved just once had more normative scores on objective psychological tests than either those who never carved or those who carved many times. The multiple carvers were the most socially popular girls. These girls tended to be absent without leave more often. The non-carvers were the least socially popular girls. The groups did not differ in recividism.

Cookson (1977) studied 48 acts of self-mutilation by 39 women over a six-month period in a prison for women in London. The average daily census was 322 women, and there was an average of 1.5 self-mutilations per week. The majority of the self-mutilations took place in the cells by cutting, mainly with glass. The incidents were spread out evenly over the course of the day and night. There seemed to be fewer incidents on Saturdays when visitors were allowed.

Self-mutilators did not differ from the general prison population in age or religion. The self-mutilators did have longer sentences (more often over one year in length) and were convicted of violent crimes. On a psychological test, the self-mutilators showed more guilt, self-criticism, acting-out of hostility, and self-directed hostility than the other prisoners. Eighty-four percent of the women had previously injured themselves. The incidents of self-mutilation did not appear to be related to the premenstrual syndrome or to overcrowding or understaffing at the prison. The incidents did cluster, suggesting an imitation effect.

Cookson found that bad news, quarrels with other inmates, and even trivial events could trigger a self-mutilation. One woman mutilated herself when her parole date was cancelled after she had told her child that she would see her on the planned day. In another case, a woman did not want to be transferred to another prison; she requested that she be allowed to stay where she was so that her husband could continue to visit her. When her request was turned down, she injured herself. Another woman was told that her husband had been in a car accident, but was given no further information. This caused her to mutilate herself.

Adolescent Self-Mutilators

Johnson (1978) found that adolescent inmates who mutilated themselves or attempted suicide differed from older inmates in their possible reasons for self-injury. The adolescents were more likely to be experiencing panic because of being placed in solitary confinement, to be making last-ditch efforts to get social support, or to be unable to face the social pressures and threats from other inmates. (Crises relating to self-evaluation, needs for staff assistance, or impulse control did not differentiate between the adolescent and older self-injurers.)

In a medium-security federal youth center, Allen (1969) studied ten youths who made cuts in their arms that were deep enough to require sutures. The cutters, who were more often white, seemed to Allen to be coming out of a depressive phase, and were clearly anxious. Allen viewed their attempts as restrained but truly suicidal acts—that is, the youths might have died had they not limited their self-destructive behavior. Their goals seemed to be a desire to escape from their peers and to manipulate the staff.

SUICIDE VERSUS SELF-MUTILATION

Menninger (1938) argued that the suicidal desire could manifest itself in many ways, consciously and unconsciously and in both direct and subtle manners. He considered behavior such as alcoholism to be *chronic* suicide since the addicted persons were killing themselves slowly, shortening their lives by their substance abuse. Similarly, Menninger viewed self-mutilation as motivated by the suicidal desire; he noted, however, that rather than destroying the complete "self," self-mutilators destroy or harm just one part of themselves, in some respects a more adaptive channeling of the suicidal desire. Menninger called this *focal suicide.*

In contrast, Walsh and Rosen (1988) have argued that self-mutilation is quite different from attempted suicide.

The goal of self-mutilation is usually to release tension. It is less lethal, more repetitive, and a more chronic problem than attempted suicide. Self-mutilators also tend to use multiple methods and to switch methods more often than do truly suicidal people.

Interestingly, although it is commonly stated by researchers of self-mutilation that self-mutilators such as wrist-cutters are not suicidal risks, there has never been a follow-up study of to ascertain their risk of completed suicide in self-mutilators in the same way that attempted suicides have been followed up. It is entirely possible that the risk of suicide is actually greater in self-mutilators than in non-mutilators. Jones (1986), for example, found that prisoners who self-mutilated also attempted suicide more often in prison than did non-mutilators. Thus, self-mutilating prisoners may be at higher risk for suicide. The self-mutilators were more assaultive in prison, had more severe disciplinary reports, and had more prior felonies. They were also more often white and had arm and wrist scars on admission. (They did not differ in sex, marital status, attempts to escape, length of sentence, intelligence test scores or age.) Just over half of the self-mutilations took place when the inmate was in isolation.

In a study of criminally insane (mainly retarded and psychopathic) female offenders in England, McKerracher and associates (1968) found that the occurrence of self-mutilation was not related to the personality traits of extraversion or neuroticism, but the self-mutilators did show more obsessive traits. The acts of self-mutilation were not related to the phase of the menstrual cycle but did cluster on weekends. McKerracher felt that the self-mutilations occurred out of frustration and boredom during leisure time when there were not enough activities to occupy the offenders.

Outside of correctional facilities, Walsh and Rosen (1988) noted that from 28 to 40 percent of self-mutilators are found to have suicidal thoughts. In a study of adolescent self-mutilators, they found that 13 percent had suicidal thoughts during the time when they self-mutilated, and 31 percent had previously attempted suicide. The suicide attempters did not differ from the non-attempters in the characteristics of their self-mutilating behavior. Among adolescent inpatients, the incidents of self-mutilation tended to cluster together over time, suggesting the role of imitation.

TREATING THE SELF-MUTILATOR

Dealing with self-mutilation is quite difficult since the aim of the self-mutilation is often to seek attention. Thus, responding to the self-mutilator rewards this aim. For example, the inmate has to be taken out of his cell in order to receive medical treatment, and Cookson (1977) noted that medicine and attention are valued in prison. Even rough or brutal attention from the custodial staff can be rewarding since it is relatively less threatening than, for example, attacks from fellow inmates. Even though self-mutilating prisoners are sometimes punished, which may involve a period of seclusion or lost good time or honor time, the rewards may outweigh the punishment.

Martinez (1980) suggested that an effort should be made to prevent the behavior by searching the prisoner and his cell carefully. The search should cover all body cavities, the hair and the bottom of the feet, as well as cracks in the wall and floor of the cell. Staff should remove all objects from their own clothes, including pens. When being moved about the facility, the inmate should be kept away from all objects. Meals should be "finger food" served on paper plates. At times of high risk, the self-mutilating inmate should be placed in a new cell that has already been thoroughly searched for mutilating implements. Albanese (1983) noted that the regular prisoners have easy access to razor blades for shaving, and the suicidal and self-mutilating prisoners usually have access to these blades at one time or another. He suggested switching to safe razors that have nonremovable blades for all prisoners.

Martinez described the self-mutilating prisoner as un-

dersocialized, with a history of substance abuse, highly dependent and with a poor self-concept which may be true of many
inmates. The self-mutilator, in addition, has an inability to
delay gratification. Often after mutilating, the inmate becomes
concerned with the bodily damage and shows signs of hypochondria. He may complain of imaginary physical problems
and show fears of infection. Martinez suggested that relaxation
exercises can help the inmate during this phase. If the symptoms reach phobic proportion, systematic desensitization may
be effective. In systematic desensitization, the client is presented with a series of stimuli, ranging from those that produce
minimal anxiety to those producing maximum anxiety. The
client is taught how to relax and, while relaxing, the least
anxiety-arousing stimulus is presented. Eventually the client
can stay relaxed in the presence of this stimulus. Then the next
stimulus in the series is presented, all the while relaxing the
client, until that stimulus can be tolerated. This continues
until, after several months, the client can face all of the stimuli
in the series without experiencing anxiety. Eventually, some
form of counseling is needed, and Martinez suggested that
cognitive therapy to change the inmate's patterns of thinking
would be effective.

CHANGING PERSPECTIVES

Wicks (1974) noted that the question usually asked by those
who work with inmates is whether a particular self-mutilating
inmate really wanted to kill himself or was he simply trying to
be manipulative. He added that true suicidal behavior is also
manipulative. The suicidal person is trying to force a change
in the environment or in the attitudes of others toward him.

Wicks suggested that correctional staff stop trying to distinguish between self-mutilation and suicide, and simply see
both extremes of behavior as attempts at self-injury. A more
useful question is, "Why is this person trying to injure himself?"
Once this question can be answered, steps can be taken to
lessen the inmate's problems.

If, for example, the inmate injures himself because he fears attack by other inmates, then he can be placed in a more secure area and given therapeutic intervention to help him learn to adjust to institutional living. The institution might also re-examine its communications procedures so that inmates can talk to the correctional staff more easily about such concerns rather than injuring themselves.

Chapter 5

Theories of Inmate Suicide

Why do prisoners commit suicide? Or to put the question more pointedly, do prisoners commit suicide for reasons that are different from those who commit suicide in the community? In order to answer this question, we must first review theories of suicide in general.

THEORIES OF SUICIDE

Physiological Theories

In the 1960s, it was commonly argued that all people were similar and had the same potential assuming that they had equal opportunities. Over the years, scholarly beliefs have gradually changed and many people now believe that human behavior is strongly determined by genes and the physiological processes they create. This current thinking is demonstrated by the tremendous amount of psychiatric research done in the

1990s that looks for possible biochemical defects in the brains of those with different psychiatric disorders.

For the major psychiatric disorders, there is some evidence for a genetic and physiological basis. For example, children who are born to schizophrenic mothers and adopted by normal mothers have a much higher incidence of schizophrenia than children who are born to normal mothers and are then adopted (Heston 1966). All the children are adopted, but the genes inherited from the schizophrenic mothers appear to increase the likelihood of schizophrenia in their children. There is, however, no sound evidence for the inheritance of suicide per se (Lester 1988a).

As far as identifying physiological defects in the brains of those with psychiatric disorders, there are some tentative theories involving the levels of various neurotransmitters in the brain. The neurotransmitters are the biochemicals responsible for the transmission of electrical impulses in the nerve cells. At the present time, the neurotransmitter dopamine is thought most likely to be the cause of schizophrenia, and serotonin the most likely cause of depressive disorders.

There has been a great deal of research into the central nervous system of those who commit suicide (together with analyses of the cerebrospinal fluid, blood and urine) but, since the majority of those who commit suicide are depressed, this research has been done to try to confirm or disconfirm the biochemical theories of depression. A recent review of this research by Lester (1988a) indicated that the neurotransmitter most likely to be involved in suicide is serotonin, but that is probably a reflection of the fact that most suicides are depressed. Thus, despite occasional claims to the contrary, there is no reasonably sound biochemical theory of suicide at present.

It must be concluded that, while genes and biochemistry probably do have an impact on the development of the major psychoses (schizophrenia and major depressions), there is no evidence that genes and biochemistry play a special role in causing suicide.

Childhood Experiences

Since suicidologists have been unable to find a physiological basis for suicide, it seems more fruitful to turn to the opposite side of the explanatory axis and examine the experiences of people. Several childhood experiences would seem to have some relevance for the appearance of later suicidal behavior, especially for young people.

First, psychiatrically disturbed parents, parents who are substance abusers (both of drugs and alcohol), and parents who are distant, neglectful or abusive seem more likely to produce suicidal offspring. It has long been noted that the loss of parents in childhood through death or divorce increases the risk of depression and suicide later in life. For example, Lester (1989d) found that half of a group of famous suicides had suffered such a loss, mainly between the ages of 6 and 14. Interestingly, Koller and Castanos (1969) have confirmed this association among prisoners in Australia. Prisoners who had attempted suicide at some time in their past had lost both parents (especially between the ages of 10 and 15) more often than other prisoners matched for age, sex, marital status and living arrangements prior to incarceration. The subsequent environment and the cause of the loss (whether due to the death of parents or abandonment) did not differentiate between the groups.

In recent years there has been a great deal of interest in the experience of physical and sexual abuse in the childhoods of suicidal people, and most of the research finds an association between abuse and later suicidality. Lester (1991a) has confirmed this association in a sample of male prisoners in Vermont. Those who had attempted suicide at some point in their past were more likely to have been physically punished and abused by their fathers than were nonsuicidal prisoners.

In these kinds of associations, it may be that loss of parents or the experience of abuse increases the risk of psychiatric disturbance, which is responsible for the increase in the risk of suicide. Lester, in his study of physical abuse, controlled for prior psychiatric disturbance in the prisoners and still found an association between physical abuse and suicide attempts. This

makes his conclusion a little stronger, but psychiatric disturbance could still be the mediating factor in the association.

Another childhood experience – having family members,
relatives or friends attempt or complete suicide – seems to play
a role in the development of later suicidality. Suicide in family
members is perhaps a sign of a genetic predisposition to psychiatric disorder in the family, which might increase the
chances of suicide in family members. But suicide in family
members or close friends also sets a precedent for suicide as a
viable option in times of stress. For example, Leicester Hemingway was a child of 14 when his father shot himself (Leicester
was home alone and discovered the body after hearing the shot)
and an adult when his brother, Ernest Hemingway, shot himself. He, too, ended up killing himself with a gun.

Situational Factors

Clarke and Lester (1989) have argued forcefully that suicide is
more likely when lethal methods are easily available. For
example, when England switched from using coal gas (which
contains a high percentage of carbon monoxide) to natural gas
(which is relatively non-toxic) for domestic use, the national
suicide rate in England decreased by about a third. They noted,
too, that people use the methods most easily available to
them – doctors use overdoses of medication, while police officers use guns and cars (both car exhaust and car crashes).
Australia decreased the use of medications for suicide by
restricting the size of prescriptions and by putting the pills in
individual plastic blisters.

The suicidal state is usually called a crisis, and this
reflects the time-limited nature of the state. People may be
intensely suicidal for a day or two, but they usually become
less suicidal in a few days. Crisis counseling is useful in getting
suicidal people through this brief period but, on the other hand,
the easy availability of a lethal method for suicide (a gun or an
adequate supply of a lethal medication) may make it more
likely that they will commit suicide.

We will see the relevance of situational factors when we discuss "suicide-proofing" jail and prison cells in Chapter 7.

Stressors

People who have psychiatric breakdowns are typically found to have experienced a great deal of recent stress, and those who commit suicide are often found to have experienced even higher levels of recent stress (Lester 1992a). Stressors may be of various kinds. A commonly used checklist for the severity of recent stress was developed by Holmes and Rahe (1967) and is shown in Figure 5-1.

Disruptions in interpersonal relationships in the recent past are frequently encountered stressors of suicides, including friction, threat of loss, and actual separation or divorce. Clearly the stress of arrest, detention, trial and sentencing, and serving time constitute major stresses, and there has been a great deal written about the stress involved in this process (such as, Johnson 1976) and its potential for precipitating suicide (such as Danto 1989), especially in jails.

Interestingly, it has been found that extra-institutional stressors often increase in intensity prior to the appearance of suicidal behavior in inmates. For example, Power and Spencer (1987) found that juvenile suicide attempters were more likely to have experienced a recent stressful event, such as rejection by a girlfriend, and Rieger (1971) found the same to be true for suicide attempters in a federal prison.

Figure 5-1.

Recent Stressful Events

What events have happened to you in the past 12 months?

Event Rank	Event Value	Happened	Your Score	
1	100	_____	_____	Death of spouse
2	73	_____	_____	Divorce
3	65	_____	_____	Marital separation
4	63	_____	_____	Jail term
5	63	_____	_____	Death of close family member
6	53	_____	_____	Personal injury or illness
7	50	_____	_____	Marriage
8	47	_____	_____	Fired from job
9	45	_____	_____	Marital reconciliation
10	45	_____	_____	Retirement
11	44	_____	_____	Health change in family
12	40	_____	_____	Pregnancy
13	39	_____	_____	Sex differences
14	39	_____	_____	Gain of new family member
15	39	_____	_____	Business readjustment
16	38	_____	_____	Change in financial state
17	37	_____	_____	Death of a close friend
18	36	_____	_____	Change in occupation
19	35	_____	_____	Change in spousal fights
20	31	_____	_____	Mortgage over $50,000
21	30	_____	_____	Foreclosure of mortgage/loan

Event Rank	Event Value	Happened	Your Score	
22	29	_____	_____	Change in work responsibility
23	29	_____	_____	Son/daughter leaving home
24	29	_____	_____	Trouble with in-laws
25	28	_____	_____	Large personal gain
26	26	_____	_____	Wife begins or stops work
27	26	_____	_____	Begin or end school
28	25	_____	_____	Change in living conditions
29	24	_____	_____	Revision of personal habit
30	23	_____	_____	Trouble with boss
31	20	_____	_____	Change in work hours/conditions
32	20	_____	_____	Change in residence
33	20	_____	_____	Change in schools
34	19	_____	_____	Change in recreation
35	19	_____	_____	Change in church activities
36	18	_____	_____	Change in social activities
37	17	_____	_____	Mortgage under $50,000
38	16	_____	_____	Change in sleeping habits
39	15	_____	_____	Change in family socializing
40	15	_____	_____	Change in eating habits
41	13	_____	_____	Vacation
42	12	_____	_____	Christmas
43	11	_____	_____	Minor violations of the law

Psychological Factors

There are several psychological characteristics that are found more frequently in suicidal people than in nonsuicidal people. Most important, suicide is much more common in those who have a psychiatric disorder. The risk is greatest for those with major affective disorders (which in the past were called depressive psychosis and manic-depressive psychosis), high in schizophrenics and those who are addicted to alcohol and drugs, a little higher in those who have anxiety disorders (which in the past were called neuroses), and least in those who are not psychiatrically disturbed.

There are also a number of personality traits and mood states that are associated with suicidality. For example, a depressed mood is associated with an increased risk of suicide. (Depression refers to a psychiatric illness, a syndrome of symptoms and a current mood.) Beck and co-workers (1974) have suggested that one particular component of the syndrome of depression symptoms is found to be more strongly associated with suicide than other components — the feeling of hopelessness (that the current unpleasant state will continue and that there is nothing good to look forward to). Subsequent research has, on the whole, confirmed this.

This association has also been confirmed by Bonner and Rich (1990), who found that suicidal ideation in male inmates was associated with the amount of stress that they experienced by being in jail and also by how depressed and hopeless they felt. Ivanoff and Jang (1991) have found that hopelessness predicted current suicidal ideation and past suicide attempts in male prison inmates. Like Bonner and Rich's study with jail inmates, Ivanoff and Jang found that the severity of recent stressful events was also associated with current suicidal ideation. Interestingly, suicidal ideation was more common in those who had prior delinquency records and who had committed a violent crime, but was not associated with the length of their sentence or the number of visitors they had while in prison.

In addition, such traits as low self-esteem, irrational thinking and poor problem-solving skills have also been found to be associated with suicidality (Lester 1992a). Impulsivity has been found to characterize some suicidal individuals.

Conclusion

The potential suicide could be portrayed as: an individual who has a genetic predisposition for biochemical defects in the brain; who grew up in a family characterized by disturbed (and suicidal) parents that may have abused the child and divorced or died; who develops a psychiatric disorder accompanied by a depressed mood, low self-esteem, irrational thinking and poor proble-solving skills; and who, when he encounters a great deal of stress in his life, lacks the resources to cope with the stress and has a lethal method for suicide easily available.

THEORIES OF INMATE SUICIDE

Winfree (1987) divided the structural causes of inmate suicide into intra-institutional and extra-institutional. Among the *intra-institutional* causes, he listed the size of the inmate population, the convicted or non-convicted status of inmates, and staffing patterns. Among the *extra-institutional* causes, he listed state funding for the custodial institutions, court orders to correct deficiencies in the institutions, and regional variations in the self-destructive tendencies of people in general.[*] A simpler dichotomy of causes asks whether suicide results from the person or the environment.

---

[*] Winfree explored the impact of measures of some of these factors on inmate suicide, but unfortunately he looked at the total number of suicides occurring in jails in each state rather than the rate of suicide. In 1982, Winfree found that the only significant predictor of the number of suicides in each state was the number of inmates!

Inmate Personality

One set of theories of inmate suicide focuses on the possibility that certain types of personalities are more likely to commit crimes and end up in prison, and these personalities are suicide-prone. Indeed, Lester (1990b) has argued that suicidal individuals may have similarities to criminals, that the same types of theories may apply to both, and that similar strategies for prevention may be useful. For example, suicides and inmates have comparable rates of psychiatric disorder, substance abuse, impulsiveness and assaultiveness.

Contagion

It is well-documented that the reporting in the press and on television of the suicide of an American celebrity (such as Marilyn Monroe) leads to an increase in the suicide rate in the following week, especially among people of a similar sex and age (Stack 1990). Thus, the appearance of suicidal behavior seems to be affected by suggestion and imitation.

Such clustering of suicides is common in America in general. Coleman (1987) has documented many such clusters, especially among teenagers. For example, Lester (1987b) explored the dynamics of three suicides among one close-knit group of five teenagers.

Only one statistical study has been reported on clustering of suicides in inmates. Niemi (1978) looked at the suicides in Finnish lockups from 1963 to 1967. He found no evidence of any spatial-temporal clustering except possibly for suicides committed within 48 hours of incarceration.

Fawcett and Marrs (1973) documented clearly the possibility of contagion. At the Cook County jail, a 45-year-old black male jumped to his death from a fourth-level tier. The next day, a 23-year-old black male jumped from the same spot, but because he hesitated, correctional staff were able to get in place to catch him as he fell. The following day, another inmate jumped and again hesitated so that the correctional staff was able to place a mattress on the floor and this saved his life.

Prison Stress

Kennedy (1984) proposed a situational hypothesis for inmate suicide. He argued that the most stressful times for an inmate are during the first few days after incarceration (when he is socialized into the inmate subculture) and just before release (when he must prepare for entry into the outside community). Entry into the inmate culture is accompanied by high levels of anxiety and depression, while entry back into outside society is accompanied by high levels of anxiety alone. Kennedy, therefore, predicted high rates of suicide only upon entry into custody and not before release because depression accompanies only entry into custody. Therefore, according to Kennedy, the new inmate's suicide is likely to be motivated by the desire to escape from an acutely intolerable situation. Kennedy theorized that this desire may be more likely in certain types of individuals. He notes that younger people and those with less education may be more present-oriented and less able to visualize and anticipate their socialization into the prison subculture or eventual release. Thus, these inmates may be especially prone to depression upon incarceration.

Kennedy added that since many of those that are newly arrested are intoxicated with alcohol, the depression of these individuals may be worse since drunkenness is often accompanied by depression and by impulsive and self-damaging behavior. Although Kennedy felt that suicide prior to release is not very common, he did note that others disagree with him and argue instead that both transitions are traumatic and increase the risk of suicide.

Hatty (1988) has presented a similar hypothesis. She pointed out that inmate suicide is evidence of the stressful nature of prison life and may be interpreted as a radical failure to adjust to imprisonment. Writers have speculated upon the mechanisms by which the characteristics of prison life increase the risk of suicide, suggesting that concepts such as anomie (a breakdown of social values) are the mediating factors.

For example, Tracy (1972) noted a high incidence of Puerto Ricans among the suicides in New York City jails and speculated that Puerto Ricans may have particular difficulty adjusting to prison life. He suggested that blacks, who have been subjected to oppression for many years, more easily direct their anger outward toward the larger white society. Puerto Ricans, on the other hand, internalize the frustration and resentment. While there may be some validity to this hypothesis, no research has yet been conducted on suicide in black and Puerto Rican inmates so that we can adequately evaluate the hypothesis.

Hatty (1988) noted the fact that suicide rates of different ethnic groups (and of male and female inmates) in prison seem be in the same relative order as the suicide rates of the same groups in the community. However, the much higher rate of suicide among inmates suggests that it is the prison situation that increases the rate of suicide in all social groups.

Payson (1975) has suggested the opposite. He noted the tremendous stresses that accompany being in prison including abandonment by family and friends, discouragement of useful activity, predation and degradation may increase the risk of suicide. Payson further added that fear of being in prison forces people to seek acceptance and membership in the informal groups that exist in prison. This increased social interaction and social bonding provides structure and meaning to every-day existence and this may decrease the risk of suicide.

While many people discuss the horrors of prison, some inmates talk of it fondly, and actually commit crimes so they may be readmitted into the prison society which they have come to enjoy (Murrell and Lester 1981). Payson argued that the continuing personal indignity and danger of the prison setting coerces depressed and suicidal individuals to accept replacements for the objects they have lost with the only available alternatives — the fellowship, friendship and group loyalty of fellow inmates. Anxiety, depression and self-destructive tend-encies may diminish during incarceration as group acceptance and assimilation take place.

This view is rather heterodox, but no less possibly correct.

Indeed, a similar phenomenon has been described in the Nazi concentration camps. While suicide was very common during the persecution and deportation of the Jews in Europe (Kwiet 1984), once in the concentration camps, inmate suicide was reported to be rare (Roden 1982).

Payson's views suggest that it may be inappropriate to compare the suicide rate of inmates with the suicide rate of the general male population of roughly the same age. Inmates have certain characteristics, such as high rates of drug addiction, poor work records, a history of criminal involvement and disrupted personal relationships. We need to ask about the suicide rate of these types of people outside of prison. For example, it is well known that suicide is more common in alcoholics and drug abusers (Lester 1992b) and in those who are unemployed (Platt 1984). Perhaps the suicide rate of such individuals is lower in prison.

THE EFFECT OF RACE

Haycock (1989a) noted that it has become accepted that suicidal behavior, both lethal and nonlethal, is more common in white and Hispanic inmates than in black inmates. Toch (1975) saw self-injurious behavior as a response to the stress of being in prison, but it is a response that is not goal-oriented. It is deviant from inmate norms and a sign of crisis. The conclusion is, therefore, that prison is less stressful for blacks than for whites and Hispanics. Johnson (1976) has suggested that this is so because prison life has norms similar to the survival norms of the black ghetto. For Hispanics, prison is stressful because of the lack of a family-centered dependency to which they are accustomed.

Haycock (1989a) argued that the conclusions of both Toch and Johnson were false. First, he suggested that self-injury may be a goal-oriented and purposive act. For example, self-injury is a form of communication with institutional and governmental authority — a means of protest, grievance or appeal, much as hunger strikes are. Haycock supported this statement by documenting how inmates educate one another on methods of self-mutilation (for example, how to swallow a razor blade without injuring the mouth and how to cut wrists with plastic or paint chips).

Haycock noted that there may be other ways of responding to crises, and the relative frequency of one single response may not be valid as a measure of the level of stress. Furthermore, since blacks have lower suicide rates in the general U.S. population, the lower rate of self-injury for black inmates may simply confirm that blacks are less likely to injure themselves by suicidal and self-injurious behaviors. Haycock also suggested that the overwhelming preponderance of white correctional officers may lead to underreporting of black self-injurious behavior.

The importance of this debate between Haycock and Toch and Johnson is that they have proposed differential intervention and prevention approaches for black and white inmates. Johnson has suggested that the use of black peers may be more beneficial for helping black inmates in crisis, and that peer support may be less useful for white inmates. Correctional staff may be able to provide better intervention methods with white inmates in crisis. Johnson also suggested that white inmates may benefit more from counseling, especially counseling that fosters self-insight, and from educational programs about the ways of prison life. Haycock views these recommendations by Johnson as a misguided interpretation of research findings and a lack of nonwhite correctional staff and researchers.

ADDITIONAL STRESSORS FOR OFFENDERS

The Disgrace of Arrest

Suicide is more likely when an individual has experienced recent stressful events. Being arrested and then charged with a crime is one possible stress, and suicide is more likely after a person is arrested and charged with a crime. Lester and Baker

(1989) have illustrated this with examples of those arrested for buying child pornography.

In recent years, in an effort to prevent the pornographic use of children, several programs have been initiated by the U.S. Customs Service and the U.S. Postal Service to catch and prosecute those who purchase child pornography. One of the programs advertised the sale of child pornography and, after a person purchased it and accepted the delivery of the photographs, they were arrested. The programs have been given various names: Operation Borderline by the Customs Service and Project Looking Glass by the Postal Service. When arresting suspects in these operations, law enforcement officers also investigated whether these men have molested children, and several convictions for child molestation have been obtained against those who had.

For Project Looking Glass, in the first 229 mail orders received, 198 controlled deliveries were made, 142 prosecutive actions were initiated as of January 1987, and 35 cases of sexual abuse of children were uncovered according to data provided by the U.S. Postal Service. Several of those arrested have fought their arrests, claiming entrapment; occasionally the defendants have won.

Several newspapers have reported that the defendants in these operations have killed themselves as a result of the arrest or conviction. Out of 162 arrested so far in Operation Looking Glass, four are known to have committed suicide. The following is one of those cases:

One day before his first court appearance on a charge of receiving child pornography, a defendant shot himself with a handgun, beside his pickup truck, on a little-used road nine miles out of town. He was found dead at 4:30 p.m. He had received a video tape showing children performing sexual acts on September 12, was indicted by a federal grand jury on October 22, and killed himself on November 2. He was 34 years old, a graduate of a technical college, and married with two sons. He had worked as a farmer for his whole life.

Lester and Baker noted that while most disapprove of

child pornography, the punishment for purchasing it should not result in death. They point to the fact that law enforcement officers should be aware of the fact that suicide is not uncommon after arrest and initial confinement in jail. Additionally, being prosecuted for a socially disapproved offense such as child pornography can be expected to lead to shame and anxiety and suicide risk for those accused of this kind of crime can be high. Despite the repugnance with which we may view such offenders, it is clearly necessary to provide counseling by skilled suicide prevention workers to those arrested for socially unacceptable crimes. In the case described above, a religious and family man in a conservative rural community was faced with acute shame as a result of his arrest, and a suicidal crisis could have been anticipated. Also, there are various crimes that other prisoners find unacceptable and child molestation is certainly one of them. The stress of being in prison and having to bear the wrath of other inmates' disgust must be extraordinarily stressful.

Overcrowding

The United States now incarcerates a greater percentage of its population than any other country. In the past decade, prison and jail populations have doubled. At the end of 1990 state prisons across the country were estimated to be 18 percent to 29 percent over capacity and federal prisons were operating at 51 percent over rated capacity (Bureau of Justice Statistics: Prisoners 1991). Jails were reported to be 104 percent over capacity (Bureau of Justice Statistics: Jail Inmates 1991). Prison systems in 42 states are presently under court order for overcrowding or unconstitutional conditions. On any given day in the United States, more than 1.2 million Americans are behind bars!

Not surprisingly, overcrowding can be a significant stressor. Innes (1987), in discussing the effects of overcrowding in U.S. prisons, has noted that from 1979 to 1984 inmate housing space in the 527 prisons he surveyed increased by only

29 percent, while the inmate population increased by 34 percent. (Correctional staff increased by 43 percent.) During this period, the number of homicides in prison decreased, while the number of suicides increased.

Lester (1990a) examined the association between suicide rates in the prisons of the 48 continental states and the percentage of inmates with their own individual cell as well as the average square footage of cell space per inmate. He found that the suicide rate was higher in states where there were more inmates in their own individual cell. This suggests that the presence of cellmates may reduce the risk of suicide. However, because Lester's study was correlational and sociological in nature, cause-and-effect conclusions cannot legitimately be drawn from it. However, his findings do suggest the usefulness of examining whether suicide is more common among prisoners who have cells to themselves than among prisoners with cellmates.

Cox and associates (1984) found that from 1967 to 1977 in Texas, as the population of prisons increased, the rate of suicide increased three times more. They also found that suicide rates were higher in the larger institutions (populations over 1400 inmates). Thus, overcrowding may very well be a mediating factor in high jail and prison suicide rates.

Other Stressors

Wicks (1972) suggested a number of precipitating events that correctional officers should look for in evaluating the suicidal potential of inmates:

1. bad news, such as sickness or death at home, rejection by family, or infidelity of the spouse

2. homosexual rape (see also Wiggs 1989)

3. no news from home

4. solitary confinement for a first-time offender

5. an unexpected sentence of unusually long duration handed down by the courts

6. guilt arising from a crime committed by the inmate which has particularly unpleasant overtones, such as the murder of a relative or close friend; also nonacceptance by other inmates because of crimes such as rape

7. a beating from an another inmate or a correctional officer

8. confinement for a long period of time in an unsentenced status

CONCLUSIONS

We have seen in this chapter that inmates are the kind of individuals who are at a higher risk for suicide even when they are not incarcerated. Assaultive and substance-abusing males are common in jails and prisons, and these types of people are known to have high suicide rates regardless of whether they are in prison or in the community. In spite of these findings, it is clear that jail and prison life produces mood states that result in stressors that increase the likelihood of suicide. It seems evident that suicide will be relatively more common in jails and prisons than in the general community. We have also seen that some of the theories of suicide discussed in this chapter have implications for helping the suicidal inmate.

Chapter 6

Screening Inmates for Suicidal Risk

The assessment of suicidality (the risk of suicide) in inmates is dependent upon the answers to three questions: (1) what is the source of the inmates who are to be assessed, (2) what is the purpose of the assessment, and (3) what is to be assessed? Let us consider each of these in turn.

THE SOURCE OF THE INMATES

We have seen that inmates are found in various institutions: police lockups, jails, juvenile detention centers, prisons and facilities for the criminally insane. These institutions may be for men or for women, they differ in security (from minimum to maximum security), they are managed by different organizations (city, county, state or federal government, and, increasingly, private companies), they sometimes serve specialized populations, such as addicted offenders or those convicted of sexual offenses, and they are located in different regions of the country (inmates found in one county or state may differ considerably from those found in other regions).

This variety in institutions means that one simple screening device or even a screening process may not be suitable for all institutions. This, in turn, leads to the conclusion that each institution (or set of similar institutions) may have to devise a screening process tailored especially to itself. This would require a good deal of time and effort, funds for the hiring of skilled research-oriented (rather than treatment-oriented) psychologists to construct the specific instruments and devise the complete screening process, and the existence of a large inmate population on which to develop and validate an assessment procedure.

This seems to be a rather daunting task, but the picture is not as bleak as it might appear. There are some generally sound screening instruments available, which, at first, might suffice for an institution until sufficient experience is accumulated to modify the screening instruments for that particular institution.

THE PURPOSE OF THE ASSESSMENT

The second issue concerns the purpose of the assessment procedure. In some cases, assessment serves little purpose. For example, very few psychotherapists find it necessary to administer psychological tests to their clients in order to provide useful psychotherapy. Psychotherapists usually find that after having several sessions with the client they acquire sufficient information to formulate a treatment plan.

To take another example, in some institutions the mental health services provided are so minimal that assessment is simply impractical; often there are too few psychologists available to adequately assess every client. However, as discussed in Chapter 1, there is one current major reason to ensure that adequate assessment occurs: the threat of civil lawsuits, if an inmate commits suicide while under treatment or while confined, should be anticipated by all facilities at all times. Institutions must be able to show that they followed appropriate assessment procedures and used the resulting information wisely in order to defend themselves against the increasing number of lawsuits and the heavy damages that may—and usually are—imposed.

THE FOCUS OF THE ASSESSMENT

The third issue concerns the focus of the assessment. Of course, it is important to assess the suicidality of inmates, but, in general, treatment procedures are not normally dependent upon the *suicidality* of the client. The treatment chosen is determined more by the psychiatric diagnosis and the family and social situation of the client. For example, a treatment plan will typically focus on how to alleviate the client's depression or how to improve relationships in his family. The degree of suicidality merely determines the urgency with which various treatment procedures are pursued (Should the inmate be transferred to the psychiatric services?) and how custodial procedures are instituted (Should the inmate be placed in a "suicide-proof" environment and monitored constantly?).

Since many correctional facilities have only minimal counseling services, if any, the major focus in these institutions is on immediate prevention of suicide in an inmate who is judged to be at high risk. However, some long-term prisons do provide intensive counseling and psychotherapeutic services, utilizing individual psychotherapy, group therapy and therapeutic communities. Suicide prevention in these institutions takes a secondary place to ongoing intensive psychological rehabilitation.

THE ASSESSMENT OF SUICIDALITY

In the 1950s, the Los Angeles Suicide Prevention Center developed a simple suicidality assessment instrument for use by counselors working with clients over the telephone. This scale still forms the basis for most suicidality assessment in suicide prevention centers, and it has some relevance here. A shortened version of this scale (prepared by Kenneth Whittemore; see Lester 1989e) is shown in Figure 6-1. Our discussion of this scale has been elaborated by several objective scales that may be used by an interviewer to supplement the clinical judgment required in the original version of the scale.

This scale has five sections. The first section is concerned with age and sex since, when the scale was developed, completed suicide was most common in elderly white males. Obviously, in an inmate population, the relevance of age as measured in this scale needs to be modified, partly because the target population is young.

Whites have the highest risk of suicide, but in some regions of the United States, such as the Southwest, Hispanic youths have a high rate, as do African American youths in some cities and native American youths on some reservations. It is useful for clinicians to be aware of the epidemiological trends for suicide in their locale.

The second section of the scale focuses on the type and severity of psychiatric disturbance. Suicide risk is greater in those with psychosis, in substance abusers and in those who are seriously depressed. These guidelines are probably valid for all populations.

The association between depression and suicidality found in adults has been replicated in inmates, as we saw in Chapter 5 (Bonner and Rich 1990; Ivanoff and Jang 1991). There are several standardized scales for the assessment of depression (Beck et al. 1961; Zung 1965). Beck and his co-workers (1974) found that one particular component of the set of depressive symptoms is very strongly associated with prior, current and future suicidality: the feeling of hopelessness. Therefore, it is important to assess hopelessness as well as depression in potentially suicidal inmates, and Beck's group (1974) developed a self-report questionnaire for measuring hopelessness.

Incidentally, the accurate diagnosis of depression can be difficult since the depression may be "masked" in young people and indicated only by atypical symptoms. Depressed young adults may be irritable, unreasonably angry and antisocial. They may experience wild mood swings and complain of boredom. Girls may become sexually promiscuous, while boys may fight and commit acts of vandalism. On the other hand, honest reporting of depression is not uncommon, and indeed Lester (1990c) has found that adolescents in high school report much higher levels of depression on self-report inventories than do college students.

The third section of the suicide assessment scale refers to recent stressors in the person's life: losses of significant others, jobs, money, prestige and status, illnesses, accidents, criminal involvement and changes in residence. The greater the recent stress, the greater the risk of suicide, especially if the level has shown a recent increase on top of an already high level. There are several scales that assess the magnitude of recent stressors (Holmes and Rahe 1967; Sarason et al. 1978), and these can provide an objective and more accurate measure.

The fourth section is concerned with suicidal behavior. If the person has recently attempted suicide, especially using a method of high lethality, if the person has a specific plan for committing suicide in the future, and if the person has the method of choice readily available, then the risk of future suicidal behavior is high. People unused to working with suicidal clients are sometimes reluctant to ask about such behaviors and plans, but this information is critical to an adequate evaluation of suicidal risk. There is no evidence that asking about suicidal preoccupation increases the risk of suicide in the client.

In order to make this part of the assessment more objective, there are standardized scales for measuring the extent of suicidal intention from interviews with those who are thinking about suicide (Beck et al. 1979) and from detailed accounts of previous suicidal attempts (Beck et al. 1976). Reynolds (1988, 1990) has developed both a scale and a semi-structured interview to assess the extent of suicidal ideation in adolescents, and these may be useful for relatively uneducated inmates.

Finally, the fifth section of the scale inquires about the availability of resources and support for the person and the attitude of those able to provide support. For example, are the significant others hostile or sympathetic?

Figure 6-1.

A Suicide Prevention Center Suicide Potential Scale

Name:_____ Age:_____ Sex:_____

Date:_____

Rater:_____ Evaluation: 1 2 3 4 5 6 7 8 9
                                                         L   M   H

This schedule attempts to rate suicide potentiality. By suicide potentiality is meant generally the possibility that the person might destroy himself, in the present or immediate future. Listed below are categories with descriptive items which have been found to be useful in evaluating suicide potentiality. The numbers in parentheses after each item suggest the most common range of values or weights to be assigned that item: 9 is the highest, or most seriously suicidal, while 1 is the lowest, or the least seriously suicidal. The rating assigned will depend on the individual case. The rater will note the range of ratings assigned to each item varies.

The rating for each of the five categories is the average of the rates assigned to the total number of items ranked within that category. (Seldom will one be able to rate every item.)

The overall suicide potentiality rating may be found by entering the weights assigned for each category below, totaling, and dividing by the number of categories rated. This number, rounded to the nearest whole number, should also be circled at the top of this page. It is this number (circled above) which represents the degree of lethality of the person being evaluated.

Category	*Rating*
A. Age and Sex	_____
B. Symptoms	_____
C. Stress	_____
D. Prior suicidal behavior and current plan	_____
E. Communication aspects, resources, and reaction of significant other(s)	_____
Total	_____
Divide by number of categories rated	_____
Average (round to nearest whole number and circle at top of page)	_____

A. Age and Sex (1-9) **Rating for Category**
   Males

   1. 50 plus (7-9)   ____
   2. 35-49 (5-7)   ____
   3. 15-34 (3-5)   ____

   Females

   4. All ages (1-3)   ____

B. Symptoms (1-9)

   5. Severe depression: sleep disorder, anorexia, weight loss, withdrawal, despondent, loss of interest, apathy (7-9) ____
   6. Feelings of hopelessness, helplessness and exhaustion (7-9) ____
   7. Disorganization, confusion, chaos, delusions, hallucination, loss of contact, disorientation (6-8) ____
   8. Alcoholism, drug addiction, homosexuality, compulsive gambling (4-8) ____
   9. Agitation, tension, anxiety (4-6) ____
   10. Guilt, shame, embarrassment (4-6) ____
   11. Feelings of rage, hostility, anger, revenge, jealousy (4-6) ____
   12. Poor impulse control, poor judgment (4-6) ____
   13. Chronic debilitating illness (5-7) ____
   14. Repeated unsuccessful experiences with doctors and/or therapists (4-6) ____
   15. Psychosomatic illness (asthma, ulcer, etc.) and/or hypochondria (chronic minor illness complaints) (1-4) ____

C. Stress and Its Occurrence (Acute vs. Chronic) (1-9)
   16. Loss of loved person by death, divorce, or separation (including possible long-term hospitalization, etc.) (5-9) ____
   17. Loss of job, money, prestige, status (4-8) ____
   18. Sickness, serious illness, surgery, accident, loss of limb (3-7) ____
   19. Threat of prosecution, criminal involvement, exposure (4-6) ____
   20. Change(s) in life, environment, setting (4-6) ____
   21. Sharp, noticeable, and sudden onset of specific stress/symptoms (1-9) ____
   22. Recurrent outbreak of similar symptoms and/or stress (4-9) ____

23. Recent increase in long-standing traits,
    symptoms/stress (4-7)   ____

D. Prior Suicidal Behavior and Current Plan (1-9)

24. Rated lethality of previous attempts (1-9)   ____
25. History of repeated threats and depression (3-5)   ____
26. Specificity of current plan and lethality of
    proposed method – aspirin, pills, poison,
    knife drowning, hanging, jump, gun (1-9)   ____
27. Availability of means in proposed method
    and specificity in time planned (1-9)   ____

**E. Resources, Communication Aspects, and Reaction
   of Significant Other(s) *(1-9)**

28. No sources of financial support (employment,
    agencies, family) (4-9)   ____
29. No personal emotional support – family and/or
    friends – available, unwilling to help (4-7)   ____
30. Communication broken with rejection of efforts
    to re-establish by both patient and others (5-7)   ____
31. Communications have internalized goal, e.g.
    declaration of guilt, feelings of worthlessness,
    blame, shame (4-7)   ____
32. Communications have interpersonalized goal,
    e.g. to cause guilt in others, to force action
    in others, etc. (2-4)   ____

Reaction of Significant Other(s)*

33. Defensive, paranoid, rejecting, punishing
    attitude (5-7)   ____
34. Denial of own or patient's need for help (5-7)   ____
35. No feeling of concern about the patient, doesn't
    understand the patient (4-6)   ____
36. Indecisive or alternating attitude-feelings of anger
    and rejection and of responsibility and desire to help
                                              (2-5) ____

*Answers gained by direct contact with the significant other(s) are often
more reliable than those gained from the patient himself.

Rarely can telephone counselors at suicide prevention centers actually complete this entire evaluation with each caller, but the areas of concern covered in the scale are typically discussed in the course of a conversation with a client. Thus, the counselor could, if need be, complete such a form on each client after hanging up.

Lettieri (1974) derived separate scales for predicting suicide in younger males, older males, younger females and older females, but his scales did not receive wide acceptance, and subsequent researchers have not pursued his idea of deriving separate scales for different demographic groups.

Suicidologists have been quite remiss in devising these kinds of instruments. There are no reliable and generally valid scales for use with other populations, and, sometimes, very little research on certain groups. For example, in a recent review of scholarly literature, Lester (1992b) found only one study on predictors of completed suicide in drug addicts, and this study was not extensive enough to provide a basis for devising a suicide screening instrument.

SCREENING INMATES: GUIDELINES

Danto (1989) noted that the first and most opportune time for screening an inmate is during intake. He suggested that it is important to have a standardized interviewing schedule with a form that either the offender or the interviewer completes. In lockups this screening should be done during the booking. In jails and prisons the screening should be done on admission.

It is useful to add information obtained from the arresting officers in the case of an offender being booked or for an inmate moving from one correctional facility to another. Information from relatives and friends is also helpful. Depending upon the clues that have been found to be reliable indicators of suicidal potential, information from family and friends about depression and suicidal preoccupation and from the arresting officers about confrontation and resistance is the type of information

that may prove valuable in an adequate screening and evaluation of an inmate. The screening instrument should include
questions or observations on the psychiatric state of the person
and suicidal behaviors, past and present.

It is not uncommon for suicidal people to have rescue
fantasies in which they hope that friends, acquaintances or
even strangers will rescue them from self-destruction. This is
not uncommon in suicidal inmates as well. Such inmates may
joke about killing themselves, write suicide notes that they
leave to be found, communicate their wish to live and be saved,
or behave in a noticeably depressed manner. These cues should
be taken seriously by staff and other inmates. Almost all
suicides are found in retrospect to have made suicidal communications, sometimes quite subtle but often quite explicit, prior
to their death. *Those who talk about suicide are more likely to
kill themselves than those who do not.*

If staff members respond helpfully to these individuals, it
indicates that someone cares, and it suggests to the inmate that
he is worthy enough to live. If they turn a deaf ear, joke and
belittle the inmate, he may feel that the staff members are
daring him to kill himself. He may thus see his self-destruction
as the result of a homicidal plan conceived by the staff.

Predictors of Suicidal Risk

From the research reviewed briefly in Chapters 3, 4 and 5,
several suggestions have been made for screening devices. The
characteristics that have been shown to lead to a high risk of
suicide in the general population may also be useful for identifying suicidal potential in inmates. For example, the rate of
suicide is higher in those testing positive for AIDS, in those
with epilepsy, and in those with terminal illness (Lester 1992a).
These characteristics may also predict suicidal risk in inmates.

Gaston (1979) suggested the following suicidal profile: (1)
male, (2) charged with nonviolent crimes against property, (3)
from a lower socioeconomic class, (4) exhibiting signs of reactive depression, (5) with a history of psychiatric problems, (6)

with a history of suicide attempts, (7) showing poor occupational adjustment, (8) undergoing withdrawal from alcohol or drugs, and (9) between age 21 and 25. However, though the items make sense, Gaston did not carry out any study of the usefulness of this checklist in an inmate population.

Similarly, Anno (1985) suggested that a history of psychiatric disturbance, a history of prior suicide attempts, and being convicted of a death-related offense were potentially useful cues, but again he did not attempt to explore the practical value of these indicators.

Hendren and Blumenthal (1989) have discussed assessment in the forensic setting, in particular, the assessment of adolescents who come to the attention of the criminal justice system. Hendren and Blumenthal listed the following risk factors for adolescent suicide: a history of suicidal threats and attempts, drug or alcohol abuse, depression, antisocial behavior, an inhibited personality, direct or indirect exposure to suicide, evidence of family dysfunction, the anniversary of a negative life event and recent stressors or losses.

It is likely that adolescents, suicidal or otherwise, who come to the attention of correctional officers are likely to have more of these risk factors than the average adolescent. Thus, are police officers to view all the adolescents they encounter as suicidal? Hendren and Blumenthal did not answer this question. The risk factors they list are those useful for adolescents in general but are not tailored to the special subgroup that their article addresses.

Changes in an inmate's behavior are also important to note. For example, inmates who have been combative or aggressive who suddenly become meek and quiet should be watched carefully. Similarly, a peaceful inmate who suddenly provokes a guard, especially if he pushes so far that he gets beaten up, should be evaluated for suicidal potential and monitored. Any change in behavior, even a lessening of depression, can signal an increase in suicide potential. (Among psychiatric patients, for example, suicide is very common after they appear to have improved, or after they are given permission to make visits to their home or are released.)

Other Areas to Explore in the Assessment of Inmate Suicidality

In previous chapters we mentioned some factors that research has shown to be predictive of suicidal behavior. Several risk factors from the young adult's life history and current situation are worthy of note. Poor academic performance and specific skill deficits are risk factors for adolescents (Rourke et al. 1989; Lester 1992), factors that are analogous to unemployment and job difficulties for adults. Another possible characteristic is the presence of risky and generally self-destructive behavior, especially in male adolescents (Lester and Gatto 1989). Chronic and debilitating illnesses are also significant as risk factors. Poor relationships with well-adjusted peers and involvement with other depressed and alienated friends (Lester 1987b) are also risk factors to watch for. Psychiatrically disturbed parents, especially if depression and a family history of suicide are present, greatly increase the risk of suicide in their children. Such a family history suggests the possibility of genetically transmitted psychiatric disorder, increases the likelihood of a dysfunctional family environment, and provides a coping style for the child to imitate. We have also noted that a history of physical and sexual abuse of children by parents is a significant factor in increasing the risk of psychological disturbance, and subsequently, suicidality (Lester 1992).

Research in the 1980s identified borderline personality disorder traits as strongly associated with suicidality (Lester 1992). Impulsivity and anger have also been implicated. The impulsivity of suicidal individuals is perhaps responsible for their susceptibility to feeling suicidal after celebrities commit suicide (Stack 1990) and for their increased risk of suicide if others in their neighborhood or school have recently committed suicide (Coleman 1987). Low self-esteem has also been found to be common in suicidal individuals and to predict subsequent suicidal behavior (Kaplan and Pokorny 1976).

Porter and Jones (1990) have devised a simple suicide potential screening checklist for inmates, which is reproduced in Figure 6-2. A longer screening form is shown in Figure 6-3.

Figure 6-2.

Suicide Potential Screening Checklist

Inmate's name _____ Comis no. _____

Date of incarceration ___/___/___ Date of assessment___/___/___
               Yr Mo Da   Yr Mo Day

Age ____   First offense ( ) Yes ( ) No

Marital status ( ) Single ( ) Married/common-law

                ( ) Separated/divorced

	VERY MUCH IN EVIDENCE	SOMEWHAT IN EVIDENCE	NOT IN EVIDENCE

Symptoms of
depression

1. Suicidal thoughts, hallucinations, or death
2. Crying
3. Depressed mood (sad, unhappy)
4. Expressions of hopelessness or helplessness about the future
5. Expressions of worthlessness
6. Loss of energy, interest, or motivation
7. Loss of appetite or recent weight loss
8. Neglect of personal appearance
9. Disturbances in normal sleep pattern
10. Loss of sexual desire
11. Loss of enjoyment

Past history	PRESENT	ABSENT

1. Recent suicide attempt or gesture (within the last year)

2. Past history of suicide gestures
   (non-life-threatening)
3. Past history of serious suicide
   attempts (life-threatening)
4. Recent death of a loved one or divorce
5. History of previous psychiatric
   treatment (inpatient or outpatient)
6. History of aggressive, violent, or
   impulsive behavior

From K.K. Porter and M.J. Jones, 1990. *American Journal of Forensic Medicine and Pathology* 11:319-323.

Figure 6-3.

Medical, Social & Psychological Booking Interview Sheet

Inmate Name_____

ID# _____ Sex _____ Marital Status _____ DOB _____

Personal Background Information

History of Street Drug Use

No _____

Yes _____ Types and amounts (light, moderate, heavy) _____

Last Drug Dose Date _____

History of Alcohol Use or Abuse

No _____

Yes _____ Types and amounts (light, moderate, heavy)_____

Psychiatric History

No _____

Yes _____

    Outpatient treatment (where & when) _____

Inpatient (where & when) _____

_____
Use of tranquilizers (what & dose & date of last dose)

_____

Current suicidal thoughts   Yes____ No____

Feelings of hopelessness   Yes____ No____

Current suicidal feelings   Yes____ No____

History of Suicidal Behavior

No ___

Yes ___ Details as to dates, methods, circumstances_____

_____

_____

Treatment of Suicide Attempts (circle types)
1. hospitalization
2. surgery
3. emergency room contact
4. medication
5. outpatient psychiatric treatment
6. all of the above
7. none of the above

Inmate's attitude about suicidal behavior (circle types)

a. regret about not being successful
b. happy to be alive
c. thoughts of death being comforting, solving problems

Family or friends' history of suicidal behavior (circle type)

a. none
b. parents
c. brothers & sisters
d. spouses
e. children
f. romantic interests
g. friends
h. co-workers

Behavioral Symptoms and Signs (circle types)

a. sleep disturbance

　b.　headaches
　c.　loss of appetite
　d.　fainting
　e.　blackouts
　f.　nightmares
　g.　bedwetting
　h.　fingernail biting
　i.　easily upset
　j.　crying
　k.　socially withdrawing from people
　l.　increased drinking
　m.　use of drugs or medications
　n.　depression or sadness
　o.　feeling hopeless
　p.　feeling less of a person

Physical Findings (circle types)

　a.　self-inflicted injury, scars on wrists, legs, neck
　b.　shortness of breath
　c.　chest pain
　d.　abdominal pain
　e.　confusion
　f.　loss of consciousness
　g.　unable to answer simple questions
　h.　verbally hostile or abusive
　i.　violent or assaultive

Signs of Severe Mental Illness (circle types)

　a.　hearing voices
　b.　seeing visions
　c.　bizarre behavior
　d.　lifeless reactions
　e.　blank stare to eyes
　f.　nontalkative at all
　g.　unusual suspiciousness
　h.　silly laughter

Other Medical History (circle types)

　a.　diabetes (sugar) – If yes, type medication _____
　b.　epilepsy (falling out spells) – If yes, type of medication

_____

　c.　cancer
　d.　liver disease

    e. heart disease
    f. high blood pressure
    g. accidental injuries

Social Stress Experience (circle type)

    a. job loss
    b. divorce
    c. marital separation
    d. death of a loved one
    e. arrest of a friend or relative
    f. loss of a business
    g. financial loss on an investment
    h. discovery of a major health problem

Previous Police Contact (circle types)

    a. felony arrest
    b. misdemeanor arrest
    c. previous lockup (if yes, when & where) _____

_____

    d. probation
    e. imprisonment
    f. parole

Interview Observations (circle types)

    a. good eye contact
    b. poor eye contact
    c. depression (hangdog or down-in-the-mouth)
    d. anger
    e. cooperativeness
    f. understood questions and gave answers well
    g. good hygiene
    h. poor hygiene
    i. heavy smoking
    j. nicotine-stained fingers
    k. pleasantness
    l. ability to appreciate being in trouble
    m. openness in answering questions
    n. odor of alcohol
    o. signs of intoxication by drugs (or alcohol)
    p. mental confusion
    q. evidence of a thought disorder (unable to follow questions or keep his thoughts straight and logical)

Arresting Officer's Statement (circle one)

  a. threats to commit suicide
  b. history of suicidal behavior
  c. family, friends, co-workers concerned about
      potential suicidal behavior
  d. use of drugs or alcohol
  e. resistance to arrest or surly behavior toward arresting officer

---

Psychiatric Diagnosis

As we mentioned above, most suicide assessment scales increase the estimate of the risk of suicide if the client is psychiatrically disturbed. Danto (1972, 1989) observed and
documented that psychiatrically disturbed individuals often
wind up in custody. He suggested that psychiatric screening
was not merely *useful* in picking up signs of psychiatric disturbance and potential suicide risk, but it was absolutely *necessary*. In fact, after enough lawsuits have been lost by
correctional institutions, psychiatric screening may become
mandatory. Danto recommended a thorough psychiatric examination, and emphasized the need for a special focus on previous psychiatric illnesses and psychiatric hospitalization, on
the inmate's personal and family history of suicidal behavior,
and on whether the inmate is isolated from family and friends.

Anno (1985) also suggested that assessing the individual's
current psychiatric state is most useful in identifying potential
suicidality in inmates. Other signs of potential suicide are
talking about suicide to others, receiving recent bad news (such
as the death of a family member), bizarre or withdrawn behavior, and expressions of extreme shame and remorse regarding
the crime that they committed.

Research on prisoners has documented a high incidence
of psychiatric disturbance. Novick and associates (1977) studied 1420 prisoners admitted to New York City prisons in a
two-week period: 21 percent were substance abusers, 13 per-

cent had a psychiatric disturbance and 5 percent had a history of attempted suicide.

Alessi and his co-workers (1984) noted a high incidence of psychiatric disorder among incarcerated juvenile serious offenders. The most common single diagnosis was borderline personality disorder (37 percent), followed by affective disorders, including depression (15 percent) and thought disorders (10 percent). A history of attempted suicide was also common in the juveniles with 61 percent making an attempt in the previous year. Suicide attempts were especially common in those with diagnoses of borderline personality disorder and affective disorder, and their attempts were more lethal than those of other juveniles. Attempts were more common in the white delinquents, but there was no sex difference.

Chiles and associates (1980) found that 23 percent of juvenile delinquents had an affective disorder and, whereas only 10 percent of the nondepressed delinquents had a history of attempted suicide, 39 percent of the depressed delinquents had such a history. The incidences of suicidal ideation were even greater—23 percent and 61 percent respectively.

In England, Taylor and Gunn (1984) found that 14 percent of prisoners remanded on criminal charges had a personality disorder, 9 percent were psychotic, 9 percent were addicts, 3 percent had a neurosis and 3 percent had an organic brain disease. In Switzerland, Harding and Zimmerman (1989) reported that 57 percent of Swiss prisoners on remand were judged to be severely disturbed on the tenth day of incarceration, a percentage that dropped to 43 percent after 60 days.

Smialek and Spitz (1978) noted that alcohol and various drugs may exacerbate depression, as may withdrawal from these drugs. Therefore, alcohol- and drug-intoxicated inmates should be considered as a greater suicidal risk.

Clearly the presence of psychiatric disturbances, including psychosis, increases the likelihood of suicide. Thus, an adequate psychiatric evaluation is crucial for preventing suicide in inmates, and for providing guidelines for necessary medications and appropriate treatment and rehabilitation. Of the psychiatric syndromes that may be present, depression may easily be missed by untrained staff. The psychiatric syndrome of depression may be evidenced not only by the presence of a depressed mood, but by many other symptoms: loss of appetite, insomnia, lethargy, restlessness and agitation, anger, self-blame and guilt, irritability and social aloofness. Correctional staff should be aware of the many symptoms of depression and should make a point of looking for them.

Physical Screening

It is essential, of course, to complete a thorough strip-down search on all inmates, and especially those suspected of being suicidal. Obviously, putting an inmate behind bars without removing *every possible* item with which he can kill himself is inexcusably negligent.

The Role of Trust

In any assessment procedure it is important for the interviewer to establish a good relationship with the client. In the case of an adolescent this should apply to family members if possible. The clinician must gather all necessary information and, if the clinician is likely to be the adolescent's therapist, should begin to develop the therapeutic alliance.

Young adults can present special problems for the clinician since they are more likely than adults to have difficulty verbalizing their thoughts and feelings. The clinician must therefore adapt the interview to the person's maturity and style. Examples of such interviews have been provided by Fremouw and his co-workers (1990).

Inmates may be especially unwilling to trust the interviewer. This distrust is understandable since the interviewer is the government's paid agent (Halleck 1972); the reason the inmate is an inmate is because he has broken the law, and the interviewer represents the law. Because of this the interviewer may not be on the inmate's side. Greist and associates (1973) developed a computer-administered interview for suicide risk assessment, and they found that many clients preferred this type of interview over one administered by a clinician. This technique should be developed further, incorporating more recent information about suicidal risk assessment.

The Usefulness of Prisoner Aides in Screening

Although mental health professionals may be more attuned to the clues that indicate a high suicidal risk, paraprofessionals are also valuable. Charle (1981b) described a program run by the New York City Department of Corrections in which inmates were recruited as suicide prevention aides. They were given a sound training program, and their job was to identify inmates who appeared to be suicidal and then to counsel them. The prisoner aides proved to be better at identifying suicidal inmates than the guards, and furthermore it was easier for the inmates to confide in the prisoner aides. One source of friction was that the guards suspected the aides of using their position to smuggle in contraband and to facilitate other infractions.

Talking to the Family

Charle (1981b) noted that relatives and family can often provide important information relevant to estimating the risk of suicide in an inmate. The family will know of prior suicide attempts and episodes of depression and can also notice changes in the inmate's behavior that a stranger would not be able to notice. Rakis and Monroe (1989) have noted, in addition, that continued contact with relatives and friends of the inmate can be helpful if they are sensitized to spot and report signs of psychological distress during their visits with the inmate or in telephone calls and letters from him.

After Screening

It is useful to post a daily list of inmates considered to be suicidal risks so that all the correctional staff are informed about potentially suicidal inmates.

CRITICISMS OF SIMPLISTIC SCREENING PROFILES

It is easy to find critics of the usefulness of screening. Stone (1984), for example, argued that psychological and psychiatric screening is too expensive, too time-consuming and simply does not work. Anno (1985) pointed out that screening instruments that use the demographic characteristics of the inmate are not very useful. For example, to put "single" or "divorced/separated" on a screening instrument does not really help weed out suicidal inmates since most inmates are single, divorced or separated. The psychiatric items are better, but the inmate's current psychiatric condition may be the most important issue to focus on. In order to do this a good rapport with the inmate must first be established and the right questions — those that elicit details of psychiatric symptoms — must be asked.

Kennedy and Hormant (1988) have also severely criticized the use of screening profiles. They noted that model profiles from the different studies at different penal institutions vary so much that it is impossible to know which one an administrator should use for his jail or prison.

Secondly, a model profile is methodologically unsound. A set of characteristics is needed that differentiate the potentially suicidal inmate from the nonsuicidal inmate. (We might note here that despite Kennedy and Hormant's claim that these studies have never been done, there have indeed been some such studies and they are mentioned in Chapter 3.) Even these sets of characteristics (suicidal versus nonsuicidal) may differ for different institutions in different regions of the country, and perhaps in different eras, a point we have already made. Each region, and perhaps each institution, may require its own set of predictors uniquely tailored to its particular inmate population.

Third, profiles or sets of characteristics simply do not work. To illustrate this, Kennedy and Hormant (1988) applied the published national jail suicide profile — white, male, 19 to 25 years of age, with an alcohol-related offense, who committed suicide within 12 hours of admission — to 80 deaths in Michigan jails and lockups. Their model suicide fit this profile exactly. Yet, looking at how well each individual fit the profile, they found that omitting sex, 32 cases (40 percent) met three or four of the four criteria, while 48 (60 percent) met two or fewer. Thus, using three out of four as the cut-off, the profile would miss 60 percent of the suicides — the so-called false negatives (judged to be nonsuicidal, but wrongly so).

Kennedy and Hormant noted that none of the published profiles or sets of characteristics had been cross-validated, that is, tested a second or third time on new samples to see if they still held true. Typically, cross-validation reduces the size of the set of reliable characteristics and reduces the efficiency of the predictors. They pointed out that none of the predictors of inmate suicide currently uses multiple regression techniques that weight the different characteristics (since some characteristics are more effective in predicting suicide than are others).

Finally, they noted that prediction is simply not effective and certainly not cost-effective. Even the best screening instruments for suicide prediction have too many false positives, in other words, individuals judged to be suicidal who are not really so. Lester (1970), for example, assumed the best; that we could predict suicide with 75 percent accuracy. This means that in an institution with 1200 inmates of whom four will commit suicide in the next year, we could identify three of those four correctly. But we will also identify 299 of the 1196 nonsuicidal inmates as suicidal. Thus, 302 inmates would have to be placed on suicide status to order to save the three lives!

To a large extent, however, these are criticisms of the use of simplistic screening profiles that are based on the social and demographic variables reported in most research, such as the profile provided for jail inmates by the National Center on Institutions and Alternatives (Hayes 1989):

> The victim was most likely to be a 22-year-old white, single male. He would have been arrested for public intoxication, the only offense leading to his arrest, and would thereby be under the influence of alcohol and/or drugs upon incarceration. Further, the victim would not have had a significant history of prior arrests. He would have been taken to an urban county jail and immediately placed in isolation for his own protection and/or surveillance. However, less than three hours after incarceration, he would be dead. He would have hanged himself with material from his bed (i.e., sheet or pillowcase). The incident would have taken place on a Saturday night in September, between the hours of midnight and 1:00 a.m. Jail staff would have found the victim, they say, within 15 minutes of the suicide. Later, jail records would indicate that the victim did not have a history of mental illness or previous suicide attempts (Hayes 1989, p. 11).

It is clear that this profile does not utilize information on psychiatric state, current and past suicidal preoccupation, recent stressors or resources and the role of significant others. Thus, it neglects four of the five areas of concern on the simple screening instrument used by suicide prevention workers. To criticize a simplistic screening device does *not* prove that a well-designed screening device and assessment procedure could not be useful.

Hence, despite these criticisms, screening *can* work. For example, Hopes and Shaull (1986) noted that, in the county jail in Cincinnati, 161 of 2000 new inmates were sent for psychiatric evaluations in a five month period. Ten of the eleven suicide attempters during this period were among those sent for evaluations. Based on these eleven suicide attempters, they found that substance abuse, suicidal ideation, hopelessness, and more than five prior suicide attempts predicted a suicide attempt in jail. By sensitizing the correctional staff to this information the number of inmates placed on suicide watch was cut from 15 per month to 7.5 per month and the number of suicide attempts was cut from 2.5 per month to 0.33 per month. Therefore, identifying some predictors of future suicidal behavior using standard psychological/psychiatric screening reduced the suicide watches and reduced the incidence of suicidal behavior.

Gaston (1979) presented some information on the number of inmates a reasonably good screening profile could identify. Based on both completed and attempted suicides in the New York City correctional system, he identified the following profile: male, Catholic, aged 21 to 25, elementary to 9th grade education, married, property crimes, sporadic employment, Hispanic, nonaddicted, reactive (rather than endogenous) depression, prior suicide attempts, angry and hallucinating. Approximately 2 percent of 78,000 inmates fit this profile. The daily population in the system was 70,000, and 300 inmates were admitted daily. Two percent of 300 is six individuals each day, which is not an unwieldy number. Gaston examined the next 18 suicides in the system and found that 16 fit the profile.

CONCLUSIONS

The assessment of suicidal risk in inmates must encompass two needs. First, institutions must be sure that they have met adequate clinical and legal standards of care in both the assessment and the management of the potentially suicidal inmate. An excellent in-depth discussion of these standards has recently been presented by Bongar (1991). It should be noted by all administrative personnel that failure to meet the appropriate standards may very likely result in the institution losing civil suits that are brought by the family of inmates who commit suicide. These suits are costly for the institution both financially and in terms of the psychological distress to the staff and the family of the inmate. O'Leary (1989) has discussed some of the legal issues facing correctional institutions over the problem of suicide in inmates. (See also Chapter 11.)

Second, mental health personnel must acquire the information necessary to plan an adequate treatment program for the inmate, to determine if treatment and rehabilitation are possible in the institution, and to assess the urgency with which suicide prevention measures must be undertaken. Planning a treatment program requires a general assessment of the psychiatric state and the social situation of the client. Deciding upon the urgency with which treatment should commence and whether suicide precautions are warranted requires careful attention to the the assessment of the prediction of suicide risk as well. It is important that mental health personnel acquaint themselves with appropriate guidelines for the assessment and management of suicidal people, such as those recently published by Fremouw and associates (1990).

Assessment can have beneficial effects for the inmates and for the institution. Cook (1991) reported on a project in which staff from the University of Minnesota assessed 110 adolescents in two county juvenile detention centers. They were given a self-report test called the Screening for Adolescent Problems and were interviewed by staff using the Children's Depression Rating Scale. If these test instruments revealed severe disturbance, the adolescents were offered face-to-face counseling and, if they accepted the offer, a crisis intervention team visited them that same evening at the detention center. Twenty-three percent of the boys and 53 percent of the girls had attempted suicide in the past, and 12 percent of the adolescents reported strong current suicidal intentions. Twenty-six adolescents were offered help, and 20 accepted. Two of the boys were eventually judged to be at high risk for suicide.

To give another example, Sperbeck and Parlour (1986) described their experiences with 87 suicidal inmates in Anchorage, Alaska. They found that the most common psychiatric diagnosis was an adjustment disorder (associated with a conduct disorder and a depressed mood). The suicidal inmates were often substance abusers and had a great deal of secondary stress (that is, apart from incarceration, such as marital and financial problems). Although the suicidal inmates received at most only brief psychotherapy as well as anti-depressant medications (which, if hoarded by the inmates can be used for committing suicide), Sperbeck and Parlour, did make some suggestions for reducing the suicidal potential. They felt, for example, that it was an error to isolate those prisoners with psychiatric diagnoses of borderline or schizoid personality disorders, those who were extremely depressed and first-timers. On the other hand, isolation was recommended for those who were diagnosed as paranoid or who appeared fearful, belligerent, predatory or provocative toward other prisoners. This latter group also responded better to interventions from the correctional staff than from mental health personnel. Thus, screening can serve a useful guidance function for correctional counselors.

Chapter 7

Facility Design

Many suggestions have been made for preventing suicide in jails and prisons by redesigning the cells and by intensifying surveillance. In this chapter we will review some of these suggestions, which include recommendations regarding enhanced supervision of inmates, perhaps one-on-one, the use of inmates as observation aides, removing dangerous items from prisoners, establishing and maintaining good watch procedures and records, and the use of restraints and seclusion if necessary (Rakis and Monroe 1989).

CELL DESIGN

We should remember first of all that the vast majority of inmate suicides are the result of hanging. It is not necessary for the victim's feet to be off the ground for death to occur. In fact, only 2 kilograms of pressure is required to obstruct the flow of blood to and from the brain. An adult's head weighs about 3 kilograms, and so a person has only to kneel, stand, sit or even lie down while his neck is a noose in order to die. If the noose is attached to a bar, in order to hang himself the inmate either quickly spread-eagles, crouches into a prayer-like kneeling position or tucks his legs underneath him to add extra weight to the end of the crudely fashioned noose. It takes about 15 minutes to induce total asphyxia, from hooking the noose and cutting off the air supply to cutting off the blood to the head. Brain damage, however, can occur within 3 minutes. Thus, cells must be examined carefully for any dangerous parts *from the floor upward.*

Stone (1990) examined 107 suicides in Texas jails and found that all but four used hanging. Cloth, shirts, and short strips of material were used in 100 of the 103 hangings. Two others used shoe laces, and one used an extension cord that was in the jail cell in violation of state jail standards.

Stone found that the most common point of attachment was the cell crossbars (35), followed by vent and window grates (21), shower rods (16) and privacy partitions (7). Stone argued that all of these points of attachment can easily be eliminated. Cell bars, grills and grates can be covered with fine mesh metal screens or clear plexiglass sheets. Shower rods and privacy partitions can be removed. He also noted that only one of the 16 shower rods used for suicide actually had a shower curtain. Stone recommended that jail administrators should spend an hour in a "suicide-proof" cell and attempt to attach their tie to something 15 or more inches from the floor.

Jordan and co-workers (1987) replaced metal double-bunk beds in the cells in a police station with a single, solid concrete sleeping bench and a flame-retardant mattress. They covered the cell bars with plexiglass which made it impossible to affix strangling materials to the bars. They recessed the ceiling lighting for the same reason. They also installed a sound and video monitoring system to supplement the hourly physical checks by the watch commander.

Atlas (1989) provided a detailed list of suggestions for redesigning cells. For already existing cells, he suggested placing scratch-resistant polycarbonate glazing on the inside of the metal bar doors, modifying the existing light fixtures, putting tamper-proof covers over ventilation openings and all protrusions, removing all electrical outlets and eliminating all exposed pipes, hooks, hinges and catches.

For new cells, Atlas suggested: ceilings 10 feet high; recessed light fixtures with polycarbonate lens coverings; no electrical outlets; fire resistant and nontoxic material for padded walls (if these are permitted by the state); rounded corners for the walls; no exposed pipes, hooks, hinges, door knobs or catches; sealing wall joints with neoprene rubber to prevent gouging through the plaster for the purpose of anchoring a hook; sliding doors to prevent barricading the door or slamming it onto staff members; solid slab beds; stainless steel toilet-sink combinations with concealed piping and outside control over water valves; and fire detectors.

Of course, to prevent all possibilities of suicide, it is also necessary to have special clothing for inmates that cannot be torn and used for suicide. Paper clothes are one possibility worth considering.

SUICIDE METHODS OTHER THAN HANGING

Not all inmates commit suicide by hanging. Cutting is sometimes used, and so care must be taken to remove sharp objects with which an inmate could cut or puncture arteries. Potentially dangerous objects, such as pens, are often present in the pockets of correctional staff, and are often around when an inmate moves about the institution. Thus, they can easily be acquired by inmates if care is not taken. It is, of course, impossible to prevent regular inmates from having access to such implements, but it is possible to remove these objects from inmates on suicide watch. However, staff must exercise great vigilance. Porter and Jones (1990) reported the case of an inmate using the lens from his eyeglasses to kill himself.

Other methods used for suicide include fire, jumping and overdosing. Fire can be prevented by removing matches and lighters and using flame-resistant materials in the isolation cells. Jumping can be prevented by fencing in the areas from which inmates might leap. Overdosing on medications can be prevented by using injections, making sure that inmates swallow any pills that they are given, or substituting medications that are less toxic. Henry (1989), for example, calculated the overdose rates per prescription in the general population for major antidepressants, and found that more recently developed antidepressants are less likely to result in suicide.

ISOLATION VERSUS COMPANIONSHIP

"Suicide-proof" cells have been described by observers as "dehumanized," and it has been suggested that placing an inmate in such a cell might actually *increase* the risk of suicide. Hunter (1988) has looked at the design of the custodial facility from the inmate perspective rather than that of the correctional staff. Rather than "suicide-proofing" the cells, Hunter has suggested humanizing them by avoiding isolation, increasing interaction with the staff, maintaining contact by having two-way windows from the custodial working area into the cells, and preventing conditions that lead to sensory deprivation in the cells. These measures are designed to make the inmate feel less isolated and deprived and, therefore, less desperate. Human contact, even between inmate and custodial staff, may serve to build up social bonds that might weaken the suicidal impulse. Atlas (1989) suggested having windows in the cells to permit an outside view and an orientation to night and day in order to help the inmate reestablish contact with the world and minimize confusion and distortion.

Anno (1985), reflecting on suicides committed in the Texas Department of Corrections, also has suggested that suicidal inmates should not be housed alone. Rather they should be given a cellmate or put in a dormitory. Not only does this provide company and the beginnings of future social networks that can help the inmate fight his depression and despair, but it also provides a supplement to staff monitoring.

MONITORING

Potentially suicidal inmates should be monitored. Adequate monitoring requires, first of all, adequate screening and classification. The institutional procedures manual should spell out clearly and precisely which inmates are to be considered at high risk for suicide.

Copeland (1989) has noted that checking in on a prisoner every 15 minutes, which was the system in operation in Dade County in the 1980s, is too infrequent because it leaves too much time available for hanging. Placing an inmate in a group is a useful adjunct to monitoring by the correctional staff but it is still not foolproof since fellow inmates have to sleep at times. Inmates considered to be at high risk for suicide can be placed in a special psychiatric unit. They should be kept under close scrutiny with audio and video monitors in the cell and on the catwalk side of the cell (so that officers can see if the inmate is tying anything to the bars of the cell).

Electronic surveillance is not reliable. Units malfunction, and repair can be delayed. Audio and video monitoring *must* be kept operational at all times. Video monitoring should also be set up to avoid blind spots in the dark corners of cells.

In addition, those whose duties include watching electronic monitors can easily miss cues by not looking at the monitor at the appropriate time or by looking but not perceiving. Thus, electronic monitoring is no substitute for eyeball monitoring in which officers visit each cell housing a potentially suicidal inmate on a regular and recorded schedule. These visits should also be "humanized" so that, rather than simply observing the inmate, the officer makes some interpersonal contact with the inmate.

In jails and police lockups, the first 24 hours appears to be the most likely time for suicide to occur, and so careful monitoring of inmates during this period might reduce the incidence of suicide.

In addition, the best times to make a serious suicide attempt are just after an officer has checked the cells or when they are distracted by other duties. Therefore, officers should be aware that these times are particularly dangerous. On the other hand, inmates who make suicide attempts just before they know that cell monitoring is due to occur are clearly crying for help, and it is important that officers respond to this appeal in an appropriate manner.

The degree of monitoring can be adjusted to the degree of suicidal risk of the inmate, and Table 7-1 illustrates one possible set of guidelines.

EMERGENCY RESPONSE

Inmate lives may be lost because medical equipment is not readily available or, when it is available, because it is malfunctioning. Medical rescue equipment (such as oxygen) should be placed conveniently in each unit of cells, and medical equipment and communication and monitoring systems should be continually checked for malfunctioning and replaced or repaired immediately. Burtch (1979) found one problem in emergency response in the rules of the prisons he studied. Those prisons prohibited a staff member from entering a cell until one or more guards were there as back-up support. Burtch noted that obtaining back-up and the necessary keys to open cells could take so much time that an inmate who has hanged himself could die before resuscitation could be attempted. It is important to respond quickly to inmates who have hanged themselves for lives can be saved. Owens (1969) reported two such inmates who were saved, and one of them was comatose for 24 hours and still lived. When an inmate is discovered hanging, the officer should have an assistant support the body and then extricate the victim, protecting the head and neck as much as possible. Recently, the Walter F. Stevens Company of Franklin, Ohio, devised a special knife to quickly cut the noose ligature. It is also called the Rescue Tool and can be worn on a belt by correctional staff and removed from its holster like a pair of handcuffs. The hooked and curved knife blade folds for safety and cuts quickly and deftly through any type of material. Officers should also be trained in first aid and, in particular, in cardiopulmonary resuscitation. Because hanging affects the airways, the blood supply to the lungs, the brain and the spinal cord, all three areas must be considered when caring for the victim.

THE AVAILABILITY OF PSYCHIATRIC STAFF

Inmates judged to be suicidal risks should be interviewed *immediately* by a suitably trained staff member, such as a psychiatric nurse or social caseworker. Danto (1989) presented the case of a young black male who was showing signs of psychotic behavior as he came down from cocaine. He threatened suicide to his mother who called the local sheriff's department. The family and the man himself asked that he be taken to a mental health facility, but because there was an outstanding warrant for his arrest for traffic offenses he was taken to the local jail. Following his booking, he complained of not being able to breathe and that there was too much noise in his cell (although it was quiet) — both possible signs of psychosis. A nurse was called and when she arrived 45 minutes later she thought he was asleep. She left to take care of some business, and he hanged himself shortly thereafter. The nurse should have been available sooner and should have evaluated the man immediately. Delay in evaluation is often grounds for a successful litigation. If this initial interviewing reveals psychopathology, then a qualified staff psychiatrist or consultant must conduct a timely evaluation of the inmate.

THE LARGER CONTEXT

Preventing suicide by designing the facility in such a way that it is more difficult for inmates to commit suicide fits into a recent trend in general suicide prevention. For the last few decades, the two major strategies for preventing suicide have been psychiatric/psychological treatment and suicide prevention centers. In the first, potentially suicidal individuals are identified and given treatment, often including medications for the underlying psychiatric disorder and psychotherapy and counseling for the underlying psychological problems. Because it is difficult to identify potentially suicidal people in the community, this strategy is used primarily with psychiatric

Table 7-1.
Guidelines for Suicide Precaution and Management

Level of Suicide Precaution	Psychiatric Assessment Tool
Level I	Those inmates who are not verbalizing or suggesting suicidal ideation but are depressed or are admitted as indicated, i.e., alcohol or drugs.
Level II	Those inmates who have suicidal ideation and who, after assessment by staff, are assessed to be in minimal danger of actively attempting suicide, i.e., impulsive by history, intoxication at booking.
Level III	Those inmates with suicidal ideation and who, after assessment by unit staff, present clinical symptoms that indicate a higher suicide potential than Level II, i.e., history of suicide attempt(s), specific suicide plans, self-injury scare, intense guilt feelings, relatives or friends who committed suicide.
Level IV	Those inmates with suicidal ideation or delusions of self-mutilation who, after assessment by unit staff, present clinical symptoms that suggest a clear intent to follow through with the plan or delusion. Also, inmates who are psychotic and depressed, violent, or who show signs of mutilation.

Table 7-1. Continued

Examples of Patient Symptoms	Supervision and Monitoring
All inmates booked who do not meet the criteria for Levels II through IV.	1) Place in 2-man or dormitory cell. 2) Check patient's whereabouts at least every 25 minutes for first 4 hours. 3) Frequent verbal contact while awake.
1) The inmate with vague suicidal ideation but without a plan. 2) The patient who is willing to make a no-suicide contract. 3) The patient with insight into existing problems.	1) Check inmate's whereabouts every 15 minutes. 2) Frequent verbal contact while awake. 3) Place in dorm cell.
1) The inmate with a concrete suicide plan. 2) The inmate who is ambivalent about making a no-suicide contract. 3) The inmate who has minimal insight into existing problem. 4) The inmate has limited impulse control.	1) Close observation, i.e., within visual range of staff while awake. Accompany to bathroom. While asleep, inmate to be in a multiple patient room. Check patient every 15 minutes while asleep and when awake. 2) Place in mental health unit if possible. 3) Psychiatric consult necessary.
1) The inmate who is currently verbalizing a clear intent to harm self. 2) The inmate who is unwilling to make a no-suicide contract. 3) The inmate who presents no insight into existing problem. 4) The inmate has limited impulse control. 5) The inmate who has attempted suicide in the recent past by a particularly lethal method, i.e., hanging, guns or carbon monoxide. 6) Command hallucinations to commit suicide.	1) One-to-one staff observation and interaction 24 hours a day or single cell near nursing station or correctional officer. 2) Antipsychotic, antidepressant and/or anti-anxiety medication. 3) Crisis worker and psychiatric intervention. 4) Must be in mental health unit.

patients who come to consult with psychiatrists in private practice, in outpatient clinics or through inpatient services. Persons having attempted suicide who come to the attention of mental health personnel can be recruited into accepting these services.

Suicide prevention centers are typically telephone counseling services that are set up in each community, usually staffed by paraprofessionals supervised by mental health professionals. They deal with clients who call the center and they use a crisis intervention model (see Chapter 9), and usually the counseling is brief and short-term.

Clarke and Lester (1989) collected the thoughts of earlier scholars on a third strategy and argued strongly for its use — namely, removing lethal methods for committing suicide from the environment. For example, in past years heating and cooking fuel was often made from coal gas and contained high levels of carbon monoxide, which kills quickly. As countries switched to natural gas (which contains almost no carbon monoxide), cooking gas became less toxic, and its use for suicide dropped dramatically. The overall suicide rate in England dropped by over 30 percent when the switch was made. It appears, then, that if their preferred method for suicide is no longer available (or not readily accessible), people seldom switch to an alternative method for suicide.

Clarke and Lester (1989) similarly documented that as more guns become available in a community, the higher will be the suicide rate by guns, that liberal prescription of medications is associated with a greater use of overdoses for suicide, and that the imposition of emission controls on car exhausts (which removes much of the carbon monoxide) leads to a reduction in the use of exhaust fumes for suicide. Critics have often argued that making it temporarily more difficult for someone to commit suicide will not reduce the suicide rate in the long run. Clarke and Lester, in contrast, showed that restricting access to lethal methods for suicide often does reduce the suicide rate. Although people could switch to an alternative method for suicide and although they could expend time and effort to acquire their preferred means (for example, waiting several months until they have accumulated a lethal dose of medication), they apparently do not.

This suggests that the suicidal state is appropriately construed as a *time-limited crisis*. Getting the suicidal person through this crisis (by putting him in a "suicide-proof" environment, by providing crisis counseling, or by making it hard to quickly acquire the lethal means for suicide) can save a life.

DISCUSSION

Some commentators are opposed to "suicide-proofing" cells and to the use of isolation and monitoring. Hayes (1983) has said that these techniques are for the convenience of jail personnel and not for the benefit of the inmate. They increase the chances that the inmate will feel depersonalized.

On the other hand, it can be useful (and is often necessary) for an institution to have "suicide-proof" cells and suicide watches available for inmates judged to be high risk. It is, of course, possible to have relatively humanized "suicide-proof" cells. Such cells can be painted with warm colors, the bed slab can be colored plastic rather than concrete, there can be music playing, correctional staff can be friendly and caring, and the inmate can be placed with a cellmate who is a trained suicide prevention worker.

Chapter 8

The Organization and the Staff

All correctional facilities must make certain that they have established policies and procedures concerning the way they deal with inmates who are housed under their roofs. Each facility is ultimately responsible for its inmates, and every care possible must be taken to ensure that appropriate procedures and standards for suicide prevention are in place and that they are written down and given to all correctional staff. Staff must become familiar with these procedures and standards and follow them at all times. These policies and procedures should cover inmate screening, staff training, booking, and referral for health assessment and classification. This has been approved by the American Medical Association, the National Sheriffs' Association, the American Corrections Association, and the Commission on Accreditation for Corrections.

Danto (1989) also urged the establishment of an in-house or consulting medical unit that maintains a degree of autonomy from the other units. The effectiveness of this medical unit should be continually monitored, evaluated and reported to the senior administrators.

Progress toward preventing inmate suicide can be made by focusing staff training on the problem of suicide and its prevention and by modifying the behavior of the correctional staff. We will examine this strategy in this chapter.

Experience in non-correctional institutions suggests that programs are most effective when *all* staff members are thoroughly trained in the policies and procedures that have been established for their particular facility. For a correctional facility, this includes the administrators, the custodial staff, the social workers, education and medical staff, the cooks and janitors — in fact, everyone.

STAFF TRAINING

Staff training for suicide prevention should focus on the skill of recognizing and responding quickly to potentially suicidal inmates. Sovronsky and Shapiro (1989) suggested that a training program should include information about suicide (why, when and how; myths and misconceptions), signs of suicidal risk, the association between substance abuse and suicide, the role of mental illness in suicide, suicide prevention screening guidelines, communication skills, suicide in the context of lockups, jails and prisons, and local procedures regarding suicidal inmates.

Danto (1989) suggested a broader syllabus covering (1) an introduction to facts and theories about suicide; (2) the psychological impact of arrest; (3) the value of a careful, thorough booking procedure; (4) screening for suicide risk; (5) the importance of proper classification; (6) crisis intervention techniques; (7) the need for the training of correctional staff; (8) what happens to the survivors, including family, friends and correctional staff after someone has committed suicide; (9) suicide litigation in the correctional setting and what constitutes required standards; and (10) clinical case presentations and psychological autopsies (that is, in-depth analyses of particular cases of inmate suicide, including the psychological state of the inmate at the time and the procedures that were followed by the facility).

Training should also include interaction techniques.

Those most able to help a suicidal individual is the person who is right there when it is obvious that suicide is imminent, and that is usually a fellow inmate or a staff member. Recent suicide prevention programs in prisons have recruited inmates to work as counselors (Charle 1991a). Not only are these individuals likely to make better counselors (it is sometimes easier for inmates to accept counseling from other inmates; they will probably tend to be more honest than with a prison representative), and in addition, because inmates tend to have greater insight into their peers, they are more likely to detect the cues that predict suicide.

Also, the regular health staff members have a great deal of contact with inmates and could (and should) be trained to recognize signs of increased suicidal potential so that they can alert the mental health staff in the institution.

Refresher courses should also be offered periodically, especially for supervisory personnel who have been promoted or hired from outside. Refresher courses every few years can benefit all staff, especially in light of the fact that new angles and ideas are developed all the time.

A complete training manual is available from the National Center on Institutions and Alternatives Information Center, 1790 30th Street, Suite 130, Boulder, Colorado 80301.

Examples of Training Programs

Ramsay and associates (1987) have described a program set up for the Canadian Correctional Service. Initially, they provided a 4-hour workshop for new recruits into the correctional service and half-day and full-day in-service courses for regular staff. Senior administrators, however, were concerned about having such short courses, and they requested a system for delivering a standard curriculum for correctional staff throughout the nation.

Initially a 4-day workshop was set up for potential trainers, including correctional officers, living-unit staff, assistant wardens, chaplains, nurses, psychologists, teachers, shop instructors and parole officers. Some of the attenders were staff specifically designated to help offenders, but other staff were also invited who seemed to be potentially good suicide prevention counselors regardless of whether such a role fit their normal job description. Potential trainees were screened for their appropriateness.

The 4-day workshop for trainers included segments on attitudes toward suicide, facts about suicide, the development of intervention skills, and techniques for coordination in multidisciplinary intervention teams.

Upon completing the 4-day course, each apprentice trainer then conducted a workshop in a correctional facility with an experienced senior trainer. Qualified trainers were then formed into teams to conduct workshops in the correctional facilities.

Ramsay noted some resistance on the part of the custodial staff to participating in the workshops. However, in anonymous evaluations of the workshops, fewer than 2 percent of the participants expressed dissatisfaction with the workshops. Some of those trained as workshop leaders expressed concerns that they might be called upon to assume counseling duties in their institutions, but this did not happen.

Ramsay noted that in those institutions where the trainers conducted workshops, the number of referrals of suicidal inmates increased, as did the number of interventions. As a result, the incidence of suicidal behavior decreased.

One interesting feature of this program is that outside consultants were used to teach the potential trainers. The final trainers were staff of the correctional facilities, and so correctional staff were trained in suicide prevention by members of their own profession. This reduced the resistance to the program. Trainers have subsequently presented the workshops to provincial correctional institutions and to non-correctional social service agencies.

Small Institutions

Large correctional facilities employ sufficient mental health staff to provide in-service training for other staff. Smaller institutions, of course, will not have such resources. Some states have set up training programs for their smaller institutions in which centrally located mental health training staff visit the different facilities to provide 2-day courses on suicide prevention.

ANALOGIES WITH HOSPITALS

Suicide among psychiatric inpatients has been of great concern to psychiatrists, and much thought has been given to the organizational factors that increase the risk of suicide in hospitalized patients (Vogel and Wolfersdorf 1987).

Among those factors suggested as suicidogenic in the hospital organization are: deficiencies in the teaching programs for staff, especially in dealing with suicidal persons, deficiencies in the supervision of staff working with patients, lack of support by the hospital administration, lack of guidelines for dealing with suicidal patients, frequent rotations or exchanges of staff especially for the long-term patients, loss of the hospital chief or senior administrators (to another institution), high turnover rate in the patients, too small or too large wards, and unexpectedly hasty moves for patients from one ward to another.

Other factors suggested as increasing the likelihood of patient suicide are: deficient social support, isolation and loneliness especially in the long-term patients, deficient security measures, lack of personnel-patient contact and control, granting premature leaves of absence (many patients commit suicide while on leave from the hospital or soon after release), too brief and insufficient treatment, forced rehabilitation and discharge, and frequent changes in treatment strategies.

Adequate treatment in an environment with well-trained

and stable staff appears to be crucial in reducing psychiatric patient suicides.

It can be seen that many of these factors can be applied to penal institutions. Of course, there has been no research yet to test the validity of these factors as predictors of increased suicide risk in inmates, but correctional administrators and staff would do well to consider these factors in their efforts to reduce inmate suicide.

IS STAFF TRAINING EFFECTIVE?

Quinlan and Motte (1990) reported an informal evaluation of a training program for correctional officers at the Santa Clara County (California) jail. The officers were given instruction in suicide prevention, how to recognize and deal with psychiatrically disturbed inmates, and how to manage assaultive inmates. The result was a reduction in assaults on officers and suicidal attempts after the program was initiated.

However, no formal evaluation of suicide prevention programs in custodial settings, with appropriate comparison settings where no suicide prevention programs have been instituted, have yet appeared in print.

However, working in a psychiatric setting, Woolley and Eichert (1941) found that changes in the patient suicide rate in their psychiatric hospital were not related to the case load of the staff or to the expansion of the hospital. They felt that the critical explanatory factor was changes in the attitudes of the staff toward suicide. Staff were educated about suicide, and the responsibility for preventing suicide was explicitly placed on those who were in contact with the patients 24 hours a day: in the case of the hospital, the nursing staff.

STAFF BEHAVIOR

Danto (1972) noted that suicide often occurs in inmates who are or who feel socially isolated. He suggested that inmate trustees should be trained in crisis counseling and invited to form patrols at night to talk to lonely inmates. Depressed and suicidal inmates could be assigned also to special units such as group dormitories where they could interact with one another more and where specially trained staff or other inmates are available. Group therapy can also be offered to inmates in this setting.

Inmates who are thinking of killing themselves often communicate their distress with direct discussion about suicide or more indirectly by showing obvious signs of depression. It is important that staff can identify and notice these cues and respond to them. As we have noted before, people who talk about and threaten suicide *are* more likely to kill themselves and be regarded as a high risk for suicide. Even a simple action such as listening to the inmate can alleviate some of his distress. Listening communicates that someone cares. Instant advice or solutions are not necessary and would usually be unrealistic anyway. But when a staff member listens and offers to think about solutions to the inmate's problems and then checks back the next day, the inmate may feel less hopeless and less isolated.

Danto also suggested that contact between families and inmates would lessen their isolation and sense of hopelessness about the future. Such contact is especially important during times of personal crisis and despair for the inmate. Many attorneys spend very little time with their inmate clients, and inmates continually request staff to call their attorney. However, for attorneys, time is money, and there is little that can be done to persuade attorneys to make themselves more available to their incarcerated clients.

At a more basic level, those who attempt to harm themselves must receive adequate medical treatment and subsequent psychiatric evaluation. Institutional physicians should be careful in prescribing medications, since these in themselves can often be lethal. Guidelines currently exist, for example, on which antidepressants are less lethal (that is, result in fewest accidental and suicidal deaths), and physicians should obviously prescribe the less lethal medication (Henry, 1989). Institutional staff, on the other hand, should make sure that inmates take the medications prescribed for them. Patients often are reluctant to take medications, find excuses not to take them, and devise ways of deceiving staff into thinking that they have taken them when in fact they have not. It is crucial not to allow this to happen; not only do the medications help the inmate, but he may also save the medication up for a future overdose.

Danto (1989) presented the case of a 15-year-old girl arrested for aggravated assault who refused to eat and showed general oppositional behavior. Placed in a psychiatric annex, she was prescribed and given 30 Norgesic Forte tablets (an analgesic, for pain) by a physician's assistant, a one-week's supply. She ingested all thirty, but when the physician's assistant was notified of this, he did nothing. She went into convulsions three hours later and soon died. Danto observed that to give a potentially lethal dose of medication to this inmate was "at best, difficult to understand." That is, of course, an understatement. It was grossly incompetent. Danto noted that the physician's assistant argued that he followed the correctional facility's policy and that he was not negligent!

In searches of inmates and their cells, inmates who are found to have concealed weapons or medications should be evaluated for self-destructive tendencies.

For the average staff member, however, it is important to accept that they have limits as rescuers. Staff have many demands made upon their time, and they are not usually trained to be effective crisis counselors. However, if the staff cares about the inmates and if they present themselves to inmates as real people, then the rescuer role may be accepted and believed. It is acceptable to be honest about one's doubts, lack of knowledge and lack of skills. If a staff member lacks real concern about others, he must be aware of this and accept this too. But despite the limits of the typical staff member, he or she can play a decisive role in reducing inmate suicide.

PSYCHOLOGICAL ANALOGIES

Psychological autopsies involve a thorough investigation and group discussion by the staff of each case of inmate suicide. The discussion should cover the psychological state of the suicide and his past history and the procedures followed by the facility in dealing with him. This exploration can lead to new or revised procedures for suicide prevention and to an increased level of skill in responding to the suicidal inmate by the staff.

Psychological autopsies also have a psychotherapeutic effect. Correctional staff who have experienced the suicide of an inmate often need emotional support themselves. They may feel guilt over the suicide, resentment toward the inmate and other emotions. Correctional staff can benefit from recognition of this stress and advice on how to cope with it. Often simple ventilation of thoughts and feelings is a great help.

Spellman and Heyne (1989) have discussed the utility of psychological autopsies for inmate suicides and suggested a format for the review, including:

1. identifying data for the suicide such as name, age, marital status and ethnicity

2. the circumstances of the suicide, including method, date, time, location, how discovered, and who discovered the body

3. the social history of the suicide, including legal problems, adjustment to incarceration and relationships with peers and family

4. the psychiatric history of the suicide, including previous suicidal behaviors, previous psychiatric problems and treatment, and current psychiatric or psychological state

5. demographic predisposing factors, including age, sex, race and age

6. psychiatric predisposing factors, including diagnosis and past psychiatric problems

7. personality of the inmate

8. history of drug or alcohol abuse

9. suicidal behaviors in suicide's family

10. precipitants for the suicide, including recent changes in the inmate's life and losses

11. recent changes in the inmate's behavior or mood

12. recent communications regarding death or suicide from the inmate

13. reactions of the staff and fellow inmates to his suicide

14. recommendations for enhancing the suicide prevention procedures of the institution that are suggested by this review

A psychological autopsy can, therefore, serve these two purposes, helping the staff cope with suicide and improving procedures so as to prevent future suicides.

Chapter 9

Counseling the Suicidal Inmate

Those with a psychiatric/psychological orientation typically propose that intensive counseling and psychotherapy are necessary for helping the suicidal inmate. For example, Haviland and Larew (1980), in their discussion of adolescent suicides in correctional facilities, argued that the number of counseling staff at juvenile correctional facilities should be greatly increased so that intensive counseling will be available to juvenile inmates. They urge not only individual counseling, but also group counseling and family therapy.

On the other hand, Kaufman (1973) has noted that the provision of adequate mental health care in certain correctional systems may simply not be feasible. For some institutions, the budget simply cannot support a counseling service. There are often other problems. For example, Kaufman had to overcome the friction between the correctional administration and the much smaller mental health staff. A large proportion of inmates were grossly disturbed, and medications had to be used extensively with these inmates to help even the less disturbed adjust to prison life. The shortage of professional and paraprofessional mental health staff meant that screening interviews were quite brief and available only to adolescents. Mental observa-

tion cells matched the worst conditions of 18th-century prisons. Many of the correctional officers were highly resistant to
inmates using what meager mental health services were available, often delivering inmates late or not at all, even sometimes
using the confidential comments made in group therapy sessions to write infraction reports!

However, Kaufman also convincingly described the stress
and burnout suffered by the correctional officers in this institution, which are compounded by the administrative incom-
petence that forces them to work many hours of overtime, with
their pay for overtime sometimes being delayed for up to a year.

DOES PSYCHOTHERAPY HELP INMATES?

In theory, counseling and psychotherapy should help dysfunctional people lead more functional lives, and so psychotherapy
ought to be useful in helping offenders both to adjust to prison
life and to lead less maladaptive lives when released. What
happens in practice?

Lipton's group (1975) reviewed all of the efforts to use
counseling and psychotherapy to help offenders and concluded that the evidence was not strongly in favor of the ability
of psychologists to turn offenders into law-abiding citizens.
However, many successful efforts were documented in their
book.

One of the members of the team, however, published a
popular article based on the book (he even appeared on CBS's
60 Minutes) and concluded, erroneously, that rehabilitation
does *not* work (Martinson 1974). Despite the fact that
Martinson's article was an irresponsible version of the full
report, the press and government officials believed him and
used his article to cut funding for counseling programs in
correctional facilities.

Martinson later tried to make amends by publishing another article, unfortunately in an obscure law journal (Martinson 1979), in which he rejected his earlier conclusion. Despite
his recantation and the appearance of several other reviews of

counseling efforts showing that rehabilitation does indeed work (Gendreau and Ross 1987), many people still believe that rehabilitation is an ineffective strategy for offenders. Thus, it is still hard to justify funding good counseling services in most correctional facilities.

Cullen and Gendreau (1992) listed counseling procedures that were effective for rehabilitating offenders, and Lester's team (1992a) documented that many of the major systems of psychotherapy have been effectively used to help offenders lead law-abiding lives. It is unquestionably true that many offenders can be helped to a positive future through counseling.

This book is concerned with the inmate's survival in jail or prison rather than afterwards — a much simpler task. Correctional philosophies may differ (ranging from punitive to rehabilitative) but, whatever the conditions of the institution, most inmates survive and some remain well-adjusted psychiatrically. Institutions can be changed (perhaps *reformed* is a more suitable term) to make them better places from a psychological point of view, and inmates can be taught survival skills. Although it is easy to find examples of overcrowded institutions where brutality abounds, it is also possible to find correctional institutions where concerned staff work hard to help inmates.

New admissions to an institution should be examined to see whether psychotropic medications are necessary, and appropriate drugs should be prescribed only under controlled conditions. Those with predisposing psychological problems and those experiencing symptoms as a result of the arrest, trial and incarceration should receive help for their problems using standard therapeutic procedures.

CAN SUICIDAL PEOPLE BE HELPED?

Most books that deal with helping suicidal clients typically focus on brief crisis counseling, and crisis counseling makes good sense for suicidal inmates. Before exploring these techniques in greater detail, it is worth noting that suicidal clients can also benefit from more long-term and well-established systems of psychotherapy (Lester 1991b).

When dealing with a suicidal crisis we suggest that the following five contiguous and overlapping guidelines be used:

1. *Make an initial evaluation regarding the security of the crisis situation.* One of the first questions that any crisis worker should ask himself is, "How much time do I have before I must make a decision regarding this person?" This question is necessary to reduce the anxiety of working with people in crisis, for most cases are not life-or-death. Through this question the crisis is placed into the perspective of time, reduces the anxiety of the crisis worker and facilitates a better atmosphere with which to deal with the person.

2. *Develop a relationship with the person in crisis.* The crisis worker's initial step is to establish a relationship with the person in crisis, and this is where person-centered therapy as developed by Carl Rogers is appropriate (Lester 1991b). Trust is an essential element of this relationship and will be characterized by the free flow of information from the client to the crisis worker. Also, the relationship requires the feeling of interest, concern and a nonjudgmental attitude, which the crisis worker will transmit to the person in crisis. A relationship is best established through a sensing and reflecting of the emotional components in the individual's life. By doing this, the person in crisis will feel that here is a person who cares and is concerned about him. This process is called "tuning in" to the feelings of the person in crisis. The more severe the crisis situation is, the less necessary it is to focus in on the emotion and the more important it is to focus cognitively on the problem the person is having and help him to develop a means of working out the problem situation. Concern for the individual can be transmitted as effectively through interested involvement with the problem he has as it can through focusing in on the emotions related to that

problem. In the more severe crisis, there is an assumption of trust in the helping individual and a willingness on the part of the client to give the trust that is necessary to obtain the assistance he needs to resolve the crisis. The less severe the crisis is, the more necessary it is to focus in on the noncognitive, nonproblem, affective element to help the person establish a basis for trust and for the free flow of information.

3. *Help the person to identify the specific problem he has.* The person in crisis is usually confused and disorganized and has difficulty defining his problems. Care must be taken to explore the individual's total field of interaction before focusing on an individual problem, as the person in crisis is often confused and his desire to work toward an immediate solution of his problem may lead the helper astray. When the problem is specified and placed into perspective, the patient will often feel relieved. At this point with the suicidal individual, it is important to evaluate the potential for suicide. If the potential is high, immediate hospitalization may be needed, although this may sometimes be averted through step 4.

4. *Assess and mobilize the client's strength and resources.* Individuals who are in crisis often feel they have no resources on which to draw and no friends to give them assistance. In their confusion and disorganization, they often overlook people who are willing to help. By examining the crisis situation and identifying individuals in his client's life space who may be able to help him, the crisis worker often locates resources that the person has forgotten, resources that can be crucial to his recovery. At the same time, the crisis worker explores with the person means by which these resources can be mobilized and used as a support network for the client during the time of crisis. In general, the client should be encouraged to do this as much as possible for himself. However, the crisis worker must be willing to accept the responsibility to assist the client in this

activity, especially during the initial stages when confusion and disorganization may be great.

5. *Develop an action plan.* A crisis is a call for action, for
    decision. It is important to include the person in crisis
    in making the plan so that he develops a commitment
    to this plan, senses its appropriateness in   terms of
    himself and his environment and makes it succeed.

Orten (1974) has suggested a useful set of ideas for working
with people in a suicidal crisis. Orten stressed that it was
essential for the counselor to keep the client in a rational,
mature and adult state of mind. Parenting the client may
encourage him to behave like a child. The best way to restore
rationality is to ask for information. The questions should be
nonthreatening at first, that is, unrelated to the problems
causing the depression. A premature rush into these areas can
make the client act in a childlike way. Once the client has
achieved some rational control over his thoughts and emotions,
he will view the world quite differently and be more able to
deal with the emotions accompanying his problems.

Suicidal people often feel helpless, and Rosenthal (1986)
has suggested strategies that can help a suicidal client experiencing such feelings. First, Rosenthal suggested having the
client sign a written contract promising to tell the crisis worker
if he feels suicidal. This shows the client that his behavior has
had an effect on one person, the therapist. Second, it is helpful
for the crisis worker to intervene in the client's immediate
environment. For example, perhaps the crisis worker can me-
diate between the inmate and the custodial staff or other
inmates or perhaps the crisis worker can call relatives and
friends of the inmate. This shows the client that the crisis
worker is on his side and that he does not have to tackle his
problems alone. It also demonstrates to the client that the
situation, though undesirable, is not catastrophic and can be
approached rationally.

Third, Rosenthal suggested having the client keep a log of
self-defeating thoughts and feelings. Unlike cognitive therapists, Rosenthal did not advocate challenging these thoughts

and changing them. Simply tabulating these thoughts lessens their frequency and impact.

Finally, Rosenthal suggested that it is important for the crisis worker to express hope that solutions are indeed possible. For example, an inmate who expects his family to desert him can be told that the crisis worker will contact them and work to prevent this. This way, despair can be reduced.

WHO SHOULD PROVIDE THE SERVICES?

One major debate is whether jails and prisons should have adequate psychiatric care facilities and staff to handle inmates with psychiatric problems, or whether penal institutions should transfer disturbed inmates to psychiatric institutions that may lack the custodial facilities appropriate for criminals.

Obviously, small institutions will not have the budget for a full-time psychiatric staff, whereas larger institutions can, and should, have such resources available. Smaller institutions can make provisions to share psychiatric resources with other smaller institutions, or they can utilize local noncorrectional psychiatric facilities.

One advantage of sharing psychiatric resources with other correctional institutions is that the psychiatric staff will be trained, not only in psychiatry, but also in correctional problems. They should, therefore, be better equipped to work with inmates. The disadvantage may be that psychiatric consultation and services may be less readily available especially in crisis situations. The use of local noncorrectional psychiatric resources reverses this. Staff from those institutions will be less familiar (and most likely less effective) with inmates, but their services may be more readily available when needed. However, there may be friction between the correctional staff and the staff of the mental health agency, and both Brooks (1988) and Schneider and his co-workers (1990) have discussed the problems facing suicide prevention center workers when dealing with the disinterest, cynicism, distrust and suspiciousness of correctional staff. (In addition, there can be problems concerning the confidentiality of information provided by inmates to the staff of outside mental health agencies.)

Because the psychiatric staff of a correctional facility is clearly working for the institution, inmates may fear (quite legitimately) that the staff has the institution's welfare at heart, and not the inmate's. Outside psychiatric staff may be trusted more by inmates, and trust is an important component in helping suicidal people. (The same dilemma exists in employee-assistance programs in industry. Outside-run programs tend to be trusted more by employees and they are therefore more often utilized.)

In suicide prevention centers, as in many other helping programs (such as counseling for rape and spouse abuse), it has been found that nonprofessionals can perform as well as and occasionally better than professionals. People who are currently in or have been in a similar situation in the past can often understand the client much better. Thus, the use of inmates to help new admissions adjust to the institution and to help those in suicidal crises makes good sense if a sufficient core of suitable aides can be recruited and trained.

This suggests that it is a good idea if one or more staff members at the correctional facility (be it lockup, jail or prison) are trained in crisis intervention so that they can select, train and supervise prisoner aides as well as working directly with inmates in suicidal crises.

SELECTION OF APPROPRIATE COUNSELORS

Severson (1991) has discussed the problems in finding the right mental health professionals for suicide prevention work in jails and prisons. Not every mental health professional is cut out to work with inmates, just as many professionals are not suited to work with suicidal clients. Thus, counselors must be hired who can work with both inmates and with suicidal crises.

The mental health staff should be thoroughly oriented to the needs of the institution. It would not be a bad idea to have them attend the same training sessions as the custodial staff.

Care must be taken also to create a partnership between the mental health and the custodial staff. In fact, the best institutional programs are those where the custodial staff is also trained in the prevailing philosophy of the counseling program. The custodial staff must come to feel that they "own" the problem of suicide and the mental health of the inmates as much as the mental health staff. Severson urged suicide prevention training for all staff members in the institution, with yearly re-training sessions at which they can discuss current problems and new ideas concerning suicide prevention and mental health care.

INMATE SUICIDE PREVENTION WORKERS

Langley (1991) has described a program in the Rhode Island Correctional Institution to use inmates as suicide prevention workers. The program trains inmates as peer counselors so that they can be the frontline people to spot and befriend potentially suicidal inmates and refer them to the professional mental health staff. They meet and talk to all new admissions to the institution, recognizing that the first few hours are often the most likely time that inmates will consider suicide.

The group meets weekly with the program director and outside consultants from the local suicide prevention center. These meetings are for the inmate aides to discuss the problems they are facing with other inmates as well as to obtain suggestions and to unburden themselves of the stress they are under, both as inmates and as suicide prevention workers.

Langley noted that inmates make ideal aides since they are tuned in to the prison grapevine and hear about the events in the lives of other inmates that might precipitate a suicidal crisis, such as bad news from a lawyer or a "Dear John" letter from a girlfriend. Inmate aides make referrals to the mental health staff and vice versa depending on the needs of the inmate in crisis. Inmate aides are available to sit with inmates in crisis during the night when necessary. In order not to attract inmates who seek personal gain from volunteering, the inmate aides receive no extra privileges for their work, save perhaps an extra recreation period in which they are expected to work as aides, and they receive no time off from their sentence.

Possible new inmate aides are suggested by the institution's staff and other inmate aides. Once the administration approves an inmate for this role, the potential aide is interviewed, and the other program aides vote on his acceptability. Final acceptance into the program requires the director's approval as well. Langley had recruited and trained 209 aides during the program's existence, most of whom had been released after their sentence had been served, and had 67 aides working in the system at the time of writing.

Langley provided the following job description:

1. Reach inmates before they become a suicidal risk.

2. Befriend inmates who are depressed and alert psychiatric, medical or psychological staff to a developing crisis.

3. Listen to inmates' problems.

4. Ask relevant questions to potentially suicidal inmates in order to assess their suicidal risk (see Chapter 6 on screening).

5. Inform new arrivals of what to expect in prison in regard to the daily routine (rules, visitation privileges, telephone calls, etc.) and where to get help.

BEREAVEMENT COUNSELING AND THE
PSYCHOLOGICAL AUTOPSY

Those who survive a suicide often have great difficulty dealing with the emotions and thoughts aroused by the death. In the penal setting, there are fellow inmates and staff as well as family and friends who must cope with these feelings. Bereavement counseling would be of great help to all of these groups.

A psychological autopsy for the inmate suicide may often begin the working through of these feelings at the same time that the institutional procedures for preventing inmate suicide and dealing with suicidal inmates are reviewed and revised. A psychological autopsy collects together all of those involved with the deceased, pieces together the series of actions leading to the suicide and tries to come to some understanding of the deceased person's emotions and thoughts prior to his suicide. This, of course, helps the staff pinpoint ways in which the suicide might have been prevented (though not all suicides can be prevented), and it also begins a working through of the feelings generated by the suicide. (See also the discussion of psychological autopsies in Chapter 8.)

DISCUSSION

We have argued here that inmates can be helped to adjust to incarceration, that counseling can facilitate rehabilitation and that suicidal people can be helped through acute or chronic suicidal crises. We have also provided some references for those who want to read more about these issues.

More pertinent to suicide prevention, we have suggested that correctional institutions ought to, at the very least, train one or more staff members in crisis intervention so that they can help inmates who appear to be in a suicidal crisis. Institutions might also consider recruiting, selecting and training other inmates who could serve as crisis counselors for suicidal inmates. In an ideal world, more complete psychiatric and counseling services would be available at all correctional facilities, but this ideal situation may be rare and our suggested program may be the best feasible alternative for right now.

Chapter 10

Institutional Programs for Suicide Prevention

It is apparent from the foregoing chapters that suicide prevention in correctional institutions is based first on screening and identifying high-risk candidates for suicide and second on keeping the suicidal risks under surveillance in a protective setting. Both parts of the overall program must function side-by-side; neither screening nor surveillance can succeed without the other.

This chapter concerns programs in different institutions that can be considered as model programs. They can serve as examples of how an effective program can be designed and how it should function.

MODEL SUICIDE PREVENTION PROGRAMS

New York State

Cox and co-workers (1988, 1989) have described a program set up in 1985 by the New York State Office of Mental Health (in conjunction with other agencies) for five counties in New York. The participants in the program included 55 local correctional facilities, the New York City Department of Corrections, 106 local police departments and 68 local mental health providers. In all, training was given to 5115 correctional and lockup staff and 370 mental health staff; 299 staff members were trained sufficiently to keep the program running. The program had four components:

1.   An 8-hour training program in suicide prevention for jail and lockup staff.

2.   Making available a resource manual for the staff of local mental health facilities to acquaint them with the correctional system.

3.   The establishment and dissemination of policy and procedure guidelines for county jail, police lockup and mental health agency personnel regarding the management of suicidal and psychiatrically disturbed inmates.

4.   Suicide prevention admission screening guidelines.

The number of suicides in the participating detention facilities declined from 30 in 1985 to only 8 in 1989, suggesting that the program was successful in reducing the suicide rate in these particular detention facilities.

The Oneida County Correctional Facility, east of Albany, New York, joined this program for suicide prevention in 1986. It houses 250 to 300 inmates and averages about 2700 bookings each year (Jail Suicide Update 3[1], 1990). All new admissions are screened by the booking deputies. The screening includes verbal reports from significant others about the inmate's behavior; a verbal behavioral report from the local police who bring the offender (one local police department administers the suicide screening instrument itself and brings the results); a complete medical screening form that includes the inmate's psychiatric history, a check of the central file for repeat offender status, and prior mental health and suicidal behavior history. The focus point of the assessment is the administration of the suicide prevention screening program (see Figure 6-2). The screening procedure is computerized and the is inmate allowed to participate by looking at the screen which seems to encourage cooperation and ease initial apprehension. The procedure takes no more than 20 minutes. If an inmate is considered to be a suicide risk, the shift commander is notified and the inmate placed in a special surveillance facility.

Inmates classified as potential suicide risks are housed in a separate block and kept under constant observation. Each officer watches from 16 to 20 inmates, making visual checks every 15 minutes. About a third of the inmates in this special housing are typically suicidal; the others are there because of psychiatric or medical problems. Suicidal inmates are housed close to the officer's desk so that monitoring can be almost continual. There are strip-cells available if needed with only a mattress and blanket where inmates wear jumpsuits, but these are rarely needed. Records are kept of all monitoring procedures and central records are updated and reviewed daily. The number of referrals for outside mental health treatment has been reduced by about one-half of the previous level since the program was introduced.

Mobile County Jail

The Mobile County Jail in Alabama books over 8000 inmates each year and holds about 150 inmates at a time (Jail Suicide Update 3[2] 1990). All new admissions are screened including a suicide risk-screening instrument. Inmates considered to be at risk of suicide are referred to the medical division where the day nurse undertakes a more intensive screening.

Suicidal inmates are asked to sign a behavioral contract not to kill themselves while incarcerated, and most agree. (This is a common tactic in the transactional analysis approach to suicidal clients; see Lester 1991b.) Inmates who refuse to sign are assigned a "buddy," one of a select group of inmates who are trained to stay with the suicide risk and converse with him but not counsel him. They work in 8-hour shifts. Suicidal behavior is reported immediately by the buddy to the correctional and nursing staff. Correctional staff also visually check the suicidal inmate every 15 minutes, and nurses visit twice a day. Normally, only one or two inmates are on the buddy system at a time and the system is instituted for only a few days (although one inmate was reportedly on it for over 4 months).

Champaign County Correctional Center

The Champaign County (Illinois) Correctional Center began to upgrade its suicide prevention program by incorporating an 8-hour combined suicide prevention and mental health awareness program into its basic training program for personnel (Jail Suicide Update 3 [3] 1990). They then adopted a medical history screening questionnaire and supplemented this with a suicide screening form for use with all new inmates. Any new admission showing signs of potential suicidal behavior or mental illness is referred immediately to the mental health staff, who are on call 24 hours a day.

The mental health staff determines the appropriate level of surveillance necessary for the inmate and housing assignment. The monitoring can range from every 30 minutes to continuous surveillance. The facility uses isolation methods for monitoring. The isolation is for nights only for inmates with a low risk of suicide and 24 hours a day for those with a high risk. Care is taken to remove all potentially lethal objects from the inmate (such as belts and sharp objects). Paper gowns are used, and medical restraints are available though rarely used. Talks with the staff indicated some disagreement about the appropriateness of isolation, with the crisis counselor preferring to place suicidal inmates in the general housing facilities.

El Paso County Detention Facilities

The suicide prevention program at the El Paso county jail began in 1983 (Jail Suicide Update 3 [4] 1991). All new admissions must complete a comprehensive psychological screening form that contains a suicide assessment component with questions about mental health, suicidal thoughts, substance abuse, current mental status and criminal history. Additional questions about suicidal preoccupation are asked by a classification officer as a double-check. Any inmate who is under the influence of drugs or alcohol is examined hourly in the intake area until a meaningful assessment can be made. Inmates in the intake area are allowed only one layer of clothes, and any clothing that might be used for suicide is removed. All admissions are monitored continuously. Suicidal inmates who can post bond are transported to the local crisis center prior to being released from custody.

For the first 48 hours, new admissions are housed in a unit that permits easy observation. Inmates judged to be at risk for suicide are placed on the lower level in view of the correctional officer, their cell doors remain open 24 hours a day, and all inmates are checked every 15 minutes.

Transfer to the mental health unit is by request or if the inmate is considered to be suicidal or mentally disturbed. The mental health unit is an open ward with no single cells. When necessary, disturbed inmates are sent to community psychiatric facilities.

All new employees of the county sheriff's office receive 12 hours of suicide prevention and crisis intervention training, and all employees of the Detention Bureau receive annual updates of suicide prevention training. Suicide statistics from the previous year are discussed, litigation issues brought up, and suicide prevention techniques reviewed. Efforts are made to increase contact between security staff and mental health staff. A review and debriefing take place after each suicidal act. A psychological autopsy procedure is in place, but to date there has been no completed suicide.

CONCLUSION

Once a commitment is made to providing a good mental health and suicide prevention program by an institution and sufficient funding provided, it is not difficult to set up adequate staff training, good suicide screening procedures, appropriate housing, and meaningful crisis intervention and psychiatric care for inmates. The programs reviewed above have illustrated the various ways in which this can be done. All of the programs have reduced the incidence of completed suicide in their institutions, and all would fare well in litigation brought against them.

Chapter 11

The Escalating Problem
of Inmate Suicide

On any given day in the United States more than 1.2 million Americans are behind bars. This extraordinary number has increased dramatically (doubled) in just the past decade. The number of women in correctional facilities has also grown greatly, tripling during this period. Almost a quarter of the black male population now spend some time in correctional institutions. All told, about 4.5 million Americans — representing 2.5 of the total population — are under correctional supervision at present. Although there are many reasons for this explosion in the number of inmates, a major cause is the recent practice of diverting psychiatrically disturbed individuals and substance abusers into the criminal justice system rather than managing them in other more appropriate facilities. The net effect of this large scale diversion has been a serious deterioration of health care in both jails and prisons, including the mental health care of psychiatrically ill and suicidal inmates. In fact, many experts believe that a true crisis now exists as a result of overcrowding and inadequate care. The mounting problem of suicide in correctional facilities is part of the crisis. What, if anything, can be done to alleviate this critical situation?

PSYCHIATRICALLY DISTURBED OFFENDERS

As noted, in recent years the penal system has been handling increasing numbers of people with psychiatric disorders (Whitmer 1980). In 1986 Metzner and Dubovsky estimated that between 12 and 24 percent of prison inmates required psychiatric treatment and that the number of inpatient beds ranged from 12 to 22 beds per 1000 inmates. Guy and co-workers (1985) found that two-thirds of those admitted to the Philadelphia prison system were psychiatrically disturbed, and 11 percent required immediate treatment. Very recent studies estimated that between 6 percent and 14 percent of the correctional population might have *major* psychiatric problems (General Accounting Office: Mentally Ill Inmates 1991a).

During the 1970s in the United States, there was a strong movement to discharge as many psychiatric patients from institutions as was legitimately possible. For example, one Oregon state hospital reduced the number of psychiatric inpatients from more than 3500 in the 1950s to about 270 in 1988 (Batten 1989). There were several reasons for this. For one thing, there was well-documented evidence of physical and mental abuse of patients in many psychiatric facilities. There were also documented cases in which people were involuntarily confined even when there was no sound reason to do so; they posed no danger to themselves or to others (Heller et al. 1984). Courts decided that psychiatric patients' civil rights could not be ignored simply because they had received a psychiatric diagnosis.

On the pragmatic side, reducing the number of psychiatric patients enabled states to cut their budgets for such facilities and thus reduce overall spending. Although, in general, taxpayers approve of providing psychiatric treatment for those clearly in need of it, they are less supportive of having to pay taxes that will enable psychiatric facilities to be built and fully staffed.

The 1980s saw a growth in the number of homeless people in America, many of whom were former psychiatric patients. Others were people who had lost their jobs and had no money with which to rent living quarters. The homeless often commit minor crimes that cause them to be arrested, thereby moving easily into the criminal justice system. It may come as no surprise that many of those living at the margins of society prefer being in prison to living on the streets. Murrell and Lester (1981) interviewed a young adult who had spent much of his life in prison. This young man observed:

> As soon as I got back outside, in about a month or so, I got back into the same thing I was doing before, to get back to jail, because I couldn't handle being on the outside for some reason....I was happy in jail for a long time. And it's not only me, because I observed a lot of people coming back for the third and fourth time to jail, in quarantine, big smiles on their faces, carrying five to ten years....I think that jail is a haven that helps people feel happy about themselves, because they're with people they like (Murrell and Lester 1981, p.132).

Thus, in the 1990s, jails and prisons are having to deal with an increasing number of psychiatrically disturbed and marginal individuals who in earlier times might have been diverted from the criminal justice system.

Because of the high number of psychiatrically disturbed individuals that are incarcerated in jails and prisons it is crucial that psychiatric services be available.

INMATES WHO ARE SUBSTANCE ABUSERS

The second major reason for the current prison population explosion is the "War on Drugs." As part of its overall effort to reduce the use of illegal drugs in the United States, in 1989 the government initiated the National Drug Control Strategy (NDCS), a plan that has had a profound effect on the correctional system. The NDCS requires mandatory minimum sentences for a variety of drug-related crimes, many of which previously would not have demanded incarceration, especially for long periods of time. The net effect of the NDCS has been severe overcrowding of correctional facilities and an extremely high percentage of inmates with drug-related problems. For example, the General Accounting Office (1991b) reports that nearly three-quarters of inmates in state prisons and two-thirds of all inmates in federal penitentiaries were substance abusers requiring treatment. Treatment, however, is provided only infrequently for incarcerated drug abusers and this is especially true in jails where treatment is virtually nonexistent.

It is a well-documented fact that drug addiction and/or psychiatric problems are conditions known to increase the risk of suicide greatly. Considering that correctional facilities are incarcerating increasing numbers of people with these problems, it is hardly surprising that the incidence of suicide is mounting.

OTHER FACTORS CONTRIBUTING
TO SUICIDE OF INMATES

Other than the problems of psychiatrically disturbed inmates and substance abusers, there are many other reasons that the suicide rate in correctional institutions is so high. As noted earlier, jail and prison populations are largely drawn from lower socioeconomic classes. They are more likely to have come from disrupted families and to have lost parents from divorce or death, more likely to have suffered physical or sexual abuse as children, more likely to be alcohol- or drug-dependent, less likely to be married, more likely to have organic brain disorders (such as epilepsy) and more likely to have maladaptive, impulsive life styles (Haycock 1991b). All of these characteristics increase the chance that a person will commit suicide.

Added to these basic problems is the stress of arrest, trial, imprisonment and the brutal experiences of incarceration. These stresses and the reactions to them affect the inmate's relationship with friends, families and lovers and can result in anxiety, depression and hopelessness — key characteristics that cause suicidal behavior.

It has been suggested that suicides in jail and prison do

not occur because of imprisonment, but because the people in these facilities are already high-risk candidates for suicide (Kennedy and Hormant 1988). Jail/prison may simply provide a convenient setting for suicide by a person who is destined to take his own life. Put differently, the question is whether suicidal inmates are people already at risk or whether they are people in risky places (Haycock 1991b). Both of these perspectives can be combined. Incarceration may exacerbate the poor life situations of many offenders, perhaps forcing them to evaluate their lives and consider suicide. On the other hand, a correctional facility may provide a good setting for suicide for a suicidal-prone individual. It is not necessary to make a firm decision about which of these views is correct or to pit one against the other. Rather, it is more useful to include both perspectives in a suicide prevention strategy. In other terms, it is important to assess the inmate carefully to identify suicidal risk and at the same time to "suicide-proof" penal facilities.

ALTERNATIVES TO INCARCERATION

There is good reason to believe that the current health crisis in correctional facilities will not be alleviated until the diversion of psychiatrically ill individuals and drug addicts to correctional facilities is stopped or at least minimized. This could be achieved if, first, those determined upon booking to have psychiatric disturbances were placed in psychiatric rather than penal institutions. Incarceration in prisons should be revised especially for even potentially disturbed offenders who have been charged with minor crimes. Not only would this reduce the inmate population dramatically, but it would help from a rehabilitative standpoint as well. Quite simply, psychiatrically disturbed offenders are unlikely to get well in jails and prisons so that when the inmate is finally discharged he takes with him the same psychiatric problems with which he entered prison. This diversion plan, however, is easier said than done. The U.S. Supreme Court would have to reverse its decision in *O'Connor v. Donaldson* (422 US 563:1975), which affirmed the rights of the mentally ill to constitutional protection against involuntary confinement unless they were judged dangerous to themselves or to others. This legal change is not likely to occur.

Another possibility is to transfer inmates who are already in prison and have psychiatric disturbances to psychiatric institutions or mental/penal institutions. But this, too, is no simple task. Payson (1975) has noted that it is increasingly difficult to transfer psychiatrically disturbed inmates to psychiatric institutions and mental/penal institutions because these facilities are also under pressure to find alternative placements for their inmates and to reduce their resident populations (Heller et al. 1984). The fact is that correctional institutions are increasingly required to take care of their own psychiatrically disturbed inmates.

The problem of stopping the diversion of drug offenders to jails and prisons also has many obstacles. Certainly, before anything can change the NDCS with its emphasis on incarceration must be reconsidered. It seems only reasonable to send those with substance abuse problems immediately to detoxification centers or provide them with other alternative rehabilitative services rather than incarcerating them in prison where they will most likely not be helped. Hayes (1983) has correctly argued that pretrial release programs would reduce the suicide rate of prisoners. He noted that in Pima County, Arizona, a 90 percent decrease in the suicide attempts and deaths was seen since the implementation of a pretrial release program. If actual diversion cannot be accomplished, the correctional system must put into action services and treatment for substance abusers. The American Jail Association notes that from 1989 to 1990 fewer than 20 percent of jails had a drug treatment program that involved paid staff and that three-quarters of all jails did not provide group therapy, drug education or referral to community drug agencies. The General Accounting Office (Drug Treatment State Prisons; New Strategy 1991c,d) found that fewer than 20 percent of state prisons provided any kind of drug treatment and that only about 1 percent of the estimated 27,000 inmates in federal prisons who have moderate to severe drug abuse problems were receiving treatment.

Diversion of psychiatric and substance abuse inmates to

alternative settings may not be any more expensive than prisons; in fact, the cost per person for caring for correctional inmates and psychiatric or inpatients may be comparable. However, this diversion would seem appropriate for it provides disturbed offenders with the rehabilitative care they clearly need. Similarly, it is well known that drug-addicted offenders who are experiencing withdrawal have a high suicide rate; therefore, these individuals should be assisted with detoxification in a prepared setting and not left alone to withdraw.

ATTITUDES TOWARD PRISON SUICIDE

Many in our society do not consider inmate suicide a problem worthy of concern. They tend to view all inmates as undeserving of sympathy or special help. Even in a society that is now showing increased concern about many social issues such as the diminishing quality of life, family values and violence on the streets, the problem of life in prison is essentially ignored. For example, there is virtually no concern about rape, assault and other victimization among inmates, but when these acts occur in non-prison societies, there is immediate public outcry.

The fact is that prisons are a part of society and inmates are part of the population. This relationship increases as the prison population grows. Recent data indicate that almost one-quarter of all black males spend some time in prison. Clearly, the total prison population is becoming a significant sector of the U.S. population; inmates cannot be treated as if they belonged to a different world. It must also be remembered that most inmates will emerge from prison to rejoin the larger society and that what happens to them while they are in prison will shape their attitudes and behavior on the outside.

In all, on humanitarian grounds alone, it is tragic to accept the premature and unnecessary loss of life, especially by suicide, even if the victim is behind bars or is going to be sentenced. Many suicidal individuals can be helped with their crises and will find constructive alternatives to ending their lives. This is also true for those in custody. Accepting suicide because someone is a prisoner is a sad mistake.

There are also pragmatic reasons for preventing inmate suicide. Lawsuits against custodial facilities and staffs are becoming more and more frequent. The suits, brought by the relatives of the deceased, usually have little difficulty in proving some form of negligence. Most of these cases are won by the plaintiffs. (The liability of prisons and jails for inmate suicide at the federal level was forcefully discussed in a 1990 article by Olivero and Roberts.)

Local governments are now faced with large financial awards against them for a high percentage of inmate suicides, to say nothing of the huge expense of defending against these claims and the increased insurance premiums they must pay for policies to protect them. These costs have proved to be a powerful motivation for suicide prevention programs in custodial facilities.

Charle (1981b) has described another type of loss to the criminal justice system from inmate suicide. He cites an example in which the city of Los Angeles lost a key witness who had turned state's evidence in the case of the so-called "Freeway Killer" who had murdered 21 young men in 1981. The witness committed suicide!

LITIGATION OVER INMATE SUICIDE

There are two general types of lawsuits that are now plaguing the correctional system. The first concerns deprivation of rights. Many of these suits have been brought by prisoners themselves, who have become increasingly aware of their rights (Hermann and Haft 1973). Cases have been won by prisoners based on the overall unlivable conditions of a jail or prison, the use of physical punishment, disciplinary confinement and the denial of medical and mental health care.

More recently, the outbreak of prison riots has led to efforts to improve prison conditions as a means of preventing these often fatal disturbances (American Correctional Association 1981). At the same time as the general public has been unwilling to adequately fund correctional facilities, they have also been ready to blame authorities for losing control over the inmates in those facilities.

The second group of suits relate to inmate suicide. Relatives of inmates who kill themselves bring suits with impunity against the correctional officers, administrators, doctors and the local or federal government. If an institution fails to prevent suicide, especially in the absence of appropriate policies and procedures for suicide prevention, they will almost always lose the resulting lawsuits. In the end, this cost is borne by the taxpayer and it seems only appropriate for all government agencies — local, state and federal — to develop effective programs to prevent suicide.

References

Adelson, L., R.W. Huntington and D.T. Reay. 1968. A prisoner is dead. *Police* 12:49-58.

Albanese, J. 1983. Preventing inmate suicide. *Federal Probation* 47(2):65-69.

Alessi, N.E., M. McManmus, A. Brickman and L. Grapentine. 1984. Suicidal behavior among serious juvenile offenders. *American Journal of Psychiatry* 141:286-287.

Allen, T.E. 1969. Patterns of escape and self-destructive behavior in a correctional institution. *Corrective Psychiatry* 15(2):50-58.

American Correctional Association. 1981. *Riots and Disturbances in Correctional Institutions*. College Park, MD: American Correctional Association.

Anno, B.J. 1985. Patterns of suicide in the Texas Department of Corrections. *Journal of Prison and Jail Health* 5:82-93.

Anson, R. 1983. Inmate ethnicity and the suicide connection. *Prison Journal* 63(1):91-99.

Anson, R. and J. Cole. 1984. Inmate suicide. *Justice Quarterly* 1:563-567.

Atlas, R. 1989. Reducing the opportunities for inmate suicide. *Psychiatric Quarterly* 60:161-171.

Backett, S.A. 1987. Suicide in Scottish prisons. *British Journal of Psychiatry* 151:218-221.

Batten, P.J. 1989. The descriptive epidemiology of unnatural deaths in Oregon's state institutions. *American Journal of Forensic Medicine and Pathology* 10:310-314.

Beck, A.T., N. Kovacs and A. Weissman. 1979. Assessment of suicide intention. *Journal of Consulting and Clinical Psychology* 47:343-352.

Beck, A.T., C.H. Ward, M. Mendelson, J. Mock and J. Erbaugh. 1961. An inventory for measuring depression. *Archives of General Psychiatry* 4:55-63.

Beck, A.T., A. Weissman, D. Lester and L. Trexler. 1974. The measurement of pessimism. *Journal of Consulting and Clinical Psychology* 42:861-865.

Beck, A.T., A. Weissman, D. Lester and L. Trexler. 1976. Classification of suicidal behavior. *Archives of General Psychiatry* 33:835-837.

Beigel, A. and H. Russell. 1972. Suicide attempts in jails. *Hospital and Community Psychiatry* 23:361-363.

Beto, D.R. and J.L. Claghorn. 1968. Factors associated with self-mutilation within the Texas Department of Corrections. *American Journal of Correction* 30(1):25-27.

Bongar, B. 1991. *The Suicidal Patient*. Washington, DC: American Psychological Association.

Bonner, R. and A.R. Rich. 1990. Risk Factors of Suicide Intention in a Jail Population. In D. Lester, ed., *Suicide '89*. Denver: American Association of Suicidology.

Bonner, R.L. and A.R. Rich. 1990. Psychosocial vulnerability, life stress, and suicide ideation in a jail population. *Suicide and Life-Threatening Behavior* 20: 213-224.

Brooks, R.P. 1988. Suicide Prevention in Corrections. In D. Lester, ed., *Suicide '88*. Denver: American Association of Suicidology.

Burtch, B.E. 1979a. Suicide in prison. *British Journal of Psychiatry* 135:90.

Burtch, B.E. 1979b. Prisoner suicide reconsidered. *International Journal of Psychiatry and the Law* 2:407-413.

Burtka, G.J., C.J. Durand and J.W. Smith. 1988. Completed Suicides in Detroit's Wayne County Jail. In D. Lester, ed., *Suicide '88*. Denver: American Association of Suicidology.

Charle, S. 1981a. Suicide in the cellblocks. *Corrections Magazine* 6(4):6-16.

Charle, S. 1981b. How to stop jail suicides. *Police Magazine* 4(6):49-55.

Chiles, J.A., M.L. Miller and G.B. Cox. Depression in an adolescent delinquent population. *Archives of General Psychiatry* 37:1178-1184.

Clarke, R.V. and D. Lester. 1989. *Suicide: Closing the Exits*. New York: Springer-Verlag.

Coleman, L. 1987. *Suicide Clusters*. Boston: Faber & Faber.

Cook, C.G. Assessment and Intervention with Incarcerated Youth. In D. Lester, ed. *Suicide '91*. Denver: American Association of Suicidology.

Cookson, H.M. 1977. A survey of self-injury in a closed prison for women. *British Journal of Criminology* 17:332-347.

Copeland, A. 1984. Deaths in custody revisited. *American Journal of Forensic Medicine and Pathology* 5:121-124.

Copeland, A. 1989. Fatal suicidal hangings among prisoners in jail. *Medicine, Science and the Law* 29:341-345.

Cosyns, P. and J. Wilmotte. 1974. Suicidal Behaviors in Belgian Penitentiaries. In N. Speyer, R.F.W. Diekstra and K. van de Loo, eds., *Proceedings of the 7th International Conference on Suicide Prevention*. Amsterdam: Swets & Zeitlinger.

Cox, J.F., G. Landsberg and M.P. Paravati. 1989. The essential components of a crisis intervention program for local jails. *Psychiatric Quarterly* 60:103-117.

Cox, J.F., D.W. McCarty, G. Landsberg and M.P. Paravati. 1988. A model for crisis intervention services within local jails. *International Journal of Law and Psychiatry* 11:391-407.

Cox, V.C., P.B. Paulkus, and G. McCain, Prison overcrowding research. *American Psychologist* 39:1148-1160.

Cullen, F.T. and P. Gendreau. 1992. The Effectiveness of Correctional Rehabilitation and Treatment. In D. Lester, M. Braswell and P. van Voorhis, eds., *Correctional Counseling*. Cincinnati: Anderson.

Danto, B.L. 1971. The suicidal inmate. *Police Chief* 30(8):61-71.

Danto, B.L. 1972. Suicide at the Wayne County jail. *Police Law Quarterly* 1(2):34-42.

Danto, B.L. 1989. The Role of the Forensic Psychiatrist in Jail and Prison Suicide Litigation. In R. Rosner and R.B. Harmon, eds., *Correctional Psychiatry*. New York: Plenum.

De Fazio, G.L. and G. Gualandri. 1990. Self-injury in Jail and Suicidal Behavior. In G. Ferrari, M. Bellini and P. Crepet, eds., *Suicidal Behavior and Risk Factors*. Bologna, Italy: Monduzzi-Editore.

DeHeer, N. and H. Schweitzer. 1985. Suicide in jail. *Corrective and Social Psychiatry* 31:71-77.

Dressler, D.M., B. Prussof, H. Hark and Shapiro, D. 1975. Clinicians' attitudes toward the suicide attempter. *Journal of Nervous and Mental Disease* 160:146-155.

Durkheim, E. 1897. *Le Suicide*. Paris: Felix Alcan.

Dyck, R.J., R.C. Bland, S. Newman and H. Orn. 1990. Attempted Suicide and Psychiatric Disorder in a Jail Sample. In D. Lester, ed., *Suicide '90*. Denver: American Association of Suicidology.

Esparza, R. 1973. Attempted and Committed Suicide in County Jails. In B. Danto, ed., *Jailhouse Blues*. Orchard Lake, MI: Epic.

Fawcett, J. and B. Marrs. 1973. Suicide at the County Jail. In B. Danto, ed., *Jailhouse Blues*. Orchard Lake, MI: Epic.

Flaherty, M.G. 1980. *An Assessment of the National Incidence of Juvenile Suicide in Adult Jails, Lockups and Juvenile Detention Centers*. Urbana: University of Illinois.

Flaherty, M.G. The national incidence of juvenile suicide in adult jails and juvenile detention centers. *Suicide and Life-Threatening Behavior* 13:85-94.

Fremouw, W. J., M. de Perczel and T.E. Ellis. 1990. *Suicide Risk*. New York: Pergamon.

Frost, R. and P. Hanzlick. 1988. Deaths in custody. *American Journal of Forensic Medicine and Pathology* 9:207-211.

Gablis, R., B. Martineau and P. Lazaro. 1988. Suicidal Factors amongst the Mariel Cuban Entrants. In D. Lester, ed., *Suicide '88*. Denver: American Association of Suicidology.

Gaston, A. W. 1979. Prisoners. In L. D. Hankoff and B. Einsidler, eds., *Suicide*. Littleton, MA: PSG.

Gendreau, P. and R. Ross. 1987. Revivification of rehabilitation. *Justice Quarterly* 4:349-409.

General Accounting Office. 1991a. Mentally Ill Inmates: Better Data Would Help Determine Protection and Advocacy Needs (GAO/GGD-91-35). Washington, DC: GAO.

General Accounting Office. 1991b. Mentally Ill Inmates: BOP Plans to Improve Screening and Care in Federal Prisons and Jails (GAO/GGD-92-13). Washington, DC: GAO.

General Accounting Office. 1991c. Drug Treatment: State Prisons Face Challenges in Providing Services (GAO/HRD-91-128). Washington, DC: GAO.

General Accounting Office. 1991d. Drug Treatment: Despite New Strategy, Few Federal Inmates Receive Treatment (GAO/HRD-91-116). Washington, DC: GAO.

Goldfarb, R. L. and L.R. Singer. 1973. *After Conviction*. New York: Simon & Schuster.

Greist, J., D. Gustafson, F. Strauss, G. Rowse, T. Laughren and J.A. Chiles. 1973. A computer interview for suicide risk prediction. *American Journal of Psychiatry* 130:1327-1332.

Griffiths, A.W. 1990. Correlates of suicidal history in male prisoners. *Medicine, Science and the Law* 30:217-218.

Guarner, J. and R. Hanzlick. 1987. Suicide by hanging. *American Journal of Forensic Medicine and Pathology* 8:23-26.

Guy, E., J. Platt, I. Zwerling and S. Bullock. 1985. Mental health status of prisoners in an urban jail. *Criminal Justice and Behavior* 12:29-53.

Halleck, S. 1972. *The Politics of Therapy*. New York: Harper & Row.

Hankoff, L.D. 1980. Prisoners. *International Journal of Offender Therapy* 24:162-166.

Harding, T. and C. Zimmerman. 1989. Psychiatric symptoms, cognitive stress and vulnerability factors. *British Journal of Psychiatry* 155:36-43.

Hatty, S.E. 1988. Suicide in gaol. *Australian Journal of Social Issues* 23:184-195.

Haviland, L.S. and B.I. Larew. 1980. Dying in jail. *Children and Youth Services Review* 2:331-342.

Haycock, J. 1989a. Race and suicide in jails and prisons. *Journal of the National Medical Association* 81:405-411.

Haycock, J. 1989b. Manipulation and suicide attempts in jails and prisons. *Psychiatric Quarterly* 60:85-98.

Haycock, J. 1991a. Crimes and misdemeanors. *Omega* 23:81-94.

Haycock, J. 1991b. Capital crimes. *Death Studies* 15:417-433.

Haycock, J. 1991c. Comparative Suicide Risk in Involuntary Confinement. In D. Lester, ed., *Suicide '91*. Denver: American Association of Suicidology.

Hayes, L.M. 1983. And darkness closes in. *Criminal Justice and Behavior* 10:461-484.

Hayes, L.M. 1989. National study of jail suicides. *Psychiatric Quarterly* 60:7-29.

Hayes, L.M. and J.R. Rowan. 1988. *National Study of Jail Suicides*. Alexandria, VA: National Center on Institutions and Alternatives.

Heilig, S.M. 1973. Suicide in Jails. In B. Danto, ed., *Jailhouse Blues*. Orchard Lake, MI: Epic.

Heller, M.A., W.H. Traylor, S.M. Ehrlich and D. Lester. 1984. A clinical evaluation of maximum security hospital patients by staff and independent psychiatric consultants. *Bulletin of the American Academy of Psychiatry and the Law* 12:85-92.

Hendren, R.L. and S.J. Blumenthal. 1989. Adolescent suicide. *Forensic Reports* 2:47-63.

Henry, A.F. and J.F. Short. 1954. *Suicide and Homicide*. New York: Free Press.

Henry, J.A. 1989. A fatal toxicity index for antidepressant poisoning. *Acta Psychiatrica Scandinavica* Suppl. 354:37-45.

Herman, M.G. and M.G. Haft. 1973. *Prisoners' Rights Sourcebook*. New York: Clark Boardman.

Heston, L. 1966. Psychiatric disorders in foster-home reared children of schizophrenic mothers. *British Journal of Psychiatry* 112:819-825.

Hlady, W.G. and J.P. Middaugh. 1988. The underrecording of suicides in state and national records, Alaska, 1983-1984. *Suicide and Life-Threatening Behavior* 18:237-244.

Hoff, H. 1973. Prevention of Suicide among Prisoners. In B. Danto, ed., *Jailhouse Blues*. Orchard Lake, MI: Epic.

Holmes, T.H. and R.H. Rahe. 1967. The social readjustment rating scale. *Journal of Psychosomatic Research* 11:213-218.

Hopes, B. and R. Shaull. 1986. Jail suicide prevention. *Corrections Today* 48(8):64-70.

Hunter, E.M. 1988. Aboriginal suicides in custody. *Australian and New Zealand Journal of Psychiatry* 22:273-282.

Innes, C.A. 1987. The effects of prison density on prisoners. *Criminal Justice Archive and Information Network* 1:3.

Ivanoff, A. and S.J. Jang. 1991. The role of hopelessness and social desirability in predicting suicidal behavior. *Journal of Consulting and Clinical Psychology* 59:394-299.

Johnson, E.H. 1973. Felon Self-mutilation. In B. Danto, ed., *Jailhouse Blues*. Orchard Lake, MI: Epic.

Johnson, R. 1976. *Culture and Crisis in Confinement*. Lexington, MA: D.C. Heath.

Johnson, R. 1978. Youth in crisis. *Adolescence* 13:461-482.

Jones, A. 1986. Self-mutilation in prison. *Criminal Justice and Behavior* 13:286-296.

Jones, D. 1976. *Health Risks of Imprisonment*. Lexington, MA: D.C. Heath.

Jordan, F.B., K. Schmeckpeper and M. Strope. 1987. Jail suicides by hanging. *American Journal of Forensic Medicine and Pathology* 8:27-31.

Kaplan, H. and A.D. Pokorny. 1976. Self-derogation and suicide. *Social Science and Medicine* 10:113-121.

Kaufman, E. 1973. Can comprehensive mental health care be provided in an overcrowded prison system? *Journal of Psychiatry and the Law* 1:243-261.

Kennedy, D.B. 1984. A theory of suicide while in police custody. *Journal of Police Science and Administration* 12:191-200.

Kennedy, D.B. and R. Hormant. 1988. Predicting custodial suicides. *Justice Quarterly* 5:441-456.

Kerkhof, A.J.F.M. 1987. Suicidal Behavior in Jails and Prisons in the Netherlands. In R. Yufit, ed., *Proceedings of the Twentieth Annual Conference.* Denver: American Association of Suicidology.

Kerkhof, A.J.F.M. and W. Bernasco. 1990. Suicidal behavior in jails and prisons in the Netherlands. *Suicide and Life-Threatening Behavior* 20:123-137.

Koller, K.M. and J.N. Castanos. 1969. Parental deprivation and attempted suicide in prison populations. *Medical Journal of Australia* 1:858-861.

Kwiet, K. 1984. The ultimate refuge: suicide in the Jewish community under the Nazis. *Leo Baeck Institute Yearbook* 29:135-167.

Lamb, H.R., R. Schock, P.W. Chen and B. Gross. 1984. Psychiatric needs in local jails. *American Journal of Psychiatry* 141:774-777.

Langley, S. 1991. Lifeline suicide prevention program. In D. Lester, ed., *Suicide '91.* Denver: American Association of Suicidology.

Lanphear, B.P. 1987. Deaths in custody in Shelby County, Tennessee, January 1970-July 1985. *American Journal of Forensic Medicine and Pathology* 8:299-301.

Le Brun, L. 1989. Characteristics of male suicide attempts in the Sacramento County jail, 1985-1987. *Jail Suicide Update* 2(4):1-4.

Lester, D. 1970. Attempts to predict suicidal risk using psychological tests. *Psychological Bulletin* 74:1-17.

Lester, D. 1982. Suicide and homicide in U.S. prisons. *American Journal of Psychiatry* 139:1527-1528.

Lester, D. 1986. Suicide and homicide on death row. *American Journal of Psychiatry* 143:559.

Lester, D. 1987a. Suicide and homicide in U.S.A. prisons. *Psychological Reports* 61:126.

Lester, D. 1987b. *Suicide as a Learned Behavior.* Springfield, IL: Charles C Thomas.

Lester, D. 1988a. *The Biochemical Basis of Suicide.* Springfield, IL: Charles C Thomas.

Lester, D. 1989a. *Questions and Answers about Suicide.* Philadelphia: The Charles Press.

Lester, D. 1989b. Personal violence (suicide and homicide) in South Africa. *Acta Psychiatrica Scandinavica* 79:235-237.

Lester, D. 1989c. *Suicide from a Sociological Perspective.* Springfield, IL: Charles C Thomas.

Lester, D. 1989d. Experience of personal loss and later suicide. *Acta Psychiatrica Scandinavica* 79:450-452.

Lester, D. 1989e. *Can We Prevent Suicide?* New York: AMS.

Lester, D. 1990a. Overcrowding in prisons and rates of suicide and homicide. *Perceptual and Motor Skills* 71:274.

Lester, D. 1990b. *Understanding and Preventing Suicide.* Springfield, IL: Charles C Thomas.

Lester, D. 1990c. Depression and suicide in college students and adolescents. *Personality and Individual Differences* 11:757-758.

Lester, D. 1991a. Physical abuse and physical punishment as precursors of suicidal behavior. *Stress Medicine* 7:255-256.

Lester, D. 1991b. *Psychotherapy for Suicidal Clients.* Springfield, IL: Charles C Thomas.

Lester, D. 1992a. *Why People Kill Themselves.* Springfield, IL: Charles C Thomas.

Lester, D. 1992b. Alcoholism and Drug Abuse. In R. Maris, A. Berman, J. Maltsberger and R. Yufit, eds., *Assessment and Prediction of Suicide.* New York: Guilford Press.

Lester, D. and G. Baker. 1989. Suicide after legal arrest. *Medicine, Science and the Law* 29(1):78.

Lester, D., A.T. Beck and B. Mitchell. 1979. Extrapolation from attempted suicides to completed suicide. *Journal of Abnormal Psychology* 88:78-80.

Lester, D., M. Braswell and P.V. Voorhis. 1992. *Correctional Counseling*. Cincinnati: Anderson.

Lester, D. and J.L. Gatto. 1989. Self-destructive tendencies and depression as predictors of suicidal ideation in teenagers. *Journal of Adolescence* 12:221-223.

Lettieri, D.J. 1986. Suicidal death prediction scales. In A.T. Beck, H.L.P. Resnik and D.J. Lettieri, eds., *The Prediction of Suicide*. Philadelphia: The Charles Press.

Lipton, D., R. Martinson and J. Wilks. 1975. *The Effectiveness of Correctional Treatment*. New York: Praeger.

Lorettu, L., A. Pittalis, M.L. Naitana, M.N. Sanna and G.C. Nivoli. 1990. Self-destructive and Suicidal Behavior and Female Homosexuality in Penal Institutions. In G. Ferrari, M. Bellini and P. Crepet, eds., *Suicidal Behavior and Risk Factors*. Bologna, Italy: Monduzzi-Editore.

Martinez, M.E. 1980. Manipulative self-injurious behavior in correctional settings. *Journal of Offender Counseling Services and Rehabilitation* 4:275-283.

Martinson, R. 1974. What works. *The Public Interest*, Spring.

Martinson, R. 1979. New findings, new views. *Hofstra Law Review* 7:243-258.

McKerracher, D.W., T. Loughnane and R.A. Watson. 1968. Self-mutilation in female psychopaths. *British Journal of Psychiatry* 114: 829-832.

Menninger, K. 1938. *Man Against Himself.* New York: Harcourt, Brace & World.

Metzner, J.L. and S.L. Dubovsky. 1986. The role of the psychiatrist in evaluating a prison mental health system in litigation. *Bulletin of the American Academy of Psychiatry and the Law* 14:89-95.

Model suicide prevention programs. *Jail Suicide Update* 3(1)1-8, 3(2):1-5, 3(3):1-6, 1990; 3(4):1-8, 1991.

Murrell, M.E. and D. Lester. 1981. *Introduction to Juvenile Delinquency*. New York: Macmillan.

Niemi, T. 1978. The time-space distances of suicides committed in the lock-up in Finland, 1963-1967. *Israel Annals of Psychiatry* 16(1):39-45.

Novick, L.F., R. Della Penna, M.S. Schwartz, E. Remmlinger and R. Loewenstein. 1977. Health status of the New York City prison population. *Medical Care* 15:205-216.

Novick, L.F. and E. Remmlinger. 1978. A study of 128 deaths in New York City correctional facilities (1971-1976). *Medical Care* 16:749-756.

O'Leary, W.D. 1989. Custodial suicide. *Psychiatric Quarterly* 60:31-71.

Olivero, J.M. and J.B. Roberts. 1990. Jail suicide and legal redress. *Suicide and Life-Threatening Behavior* 20:138-147.

Orten, J.D. 1969. A transactional approach to suicide prevention. *Clinical Social Work Journal* 2:57-63.

Owens, D. 1969. Neuromuscular sequelae of hanging. *Corrective and Social Psychiatry* 15(3):91-95.

Payson, H.E. 1975. Suicide among males in prison. *Bulletin of the American Academy of Psychiatry and the Law* 3:152-161.

Pittalis, A., L. Lorettu, M.N. Sanna and G.C. Nivoli. 1990. Suicide and Attempted Suicide in Penal Institutions. In G. Ferrari, M. Bellini and P. Crepet, eds. *Suicidal Behavior and Risk Factors*. Bologna, Italy: Monduzzi-Editore.

Platt, S. 1984. Unemployment and suicidal behavior. *Social Science and Medicine* 19:93-115.

Porter, K.K. and M.J. Jones. 1990. Wrist slashing in a detention center. *American Journal of Forensic Medicine and Pathology* 11:319-323.

Pounder, D.J. 1986. Death behind bars. *Medicine, Science and the Law* 26:207-213.

Power, K.G. and A.P. Spencer. 1987. Parasuicidal behavior of detained Scottish young offenders. *International Journal of Offender Therapy* 31:227-235.

Quinlan, J. and E. Motte. 1990. Psychiatric training for officers. *American Jails* 4(4):22-25.

Rakis, J. and R. Monroe. 1989. Monitoring and managing the suicidal prisoner. *Psychiatric Quarterly* 60:151-160.

Ramsay, R.F., B.L. Tanney and C.A. Searle. 1987. Suicide prevention in high-risk prison populations. *Canadian Journal of Criminology* 29:295-307.

Reynolds, W.M. 1988. *Suicidal Ideation Questionnaire*. Odessa, FL: Psychological Assessment Resources.

Reynolds, W.M. 1990. Development of a semistructured clinical interview for suicidal behavior in adolescents. *Psychological Assessment* 2:382-390.

Richert, J.P. 1974. Some observations on suicides in French penal institutions. *Case and Comment* 79(6):20.

Rieger, W. 1971. Suicide attempts in a federal prison. *Archives of General Psychiatry* 24:532-535.

Roden, R.G. 1982. Suicide and holocaust survivors. *Israel Journal of Psychiatry* 19:129-135.

Rosenthal, H. 1986. The learned helplessness syndrome. *Emotional First Aid* 3(2):5-8.

Ross, R., H. McKay, W. Palmer and C. Kenny. 1978. Self-mutilation in adolescent female offenders. *Canadian Journal of Criminology* 20:375-392.

Rourke, B., G. Young and A. Leenaars. 1989. A childhood learning disability that predisposes those afflicted to adolescent and adult depression and suicide risk. *Journal of Learning Disabilities* 22:169-175.

Salive, M.E., G.S. Smith and T.F. Brewer. 1989. Suicide mortality in the Maryland state prison system, 1979 through 1987. *Journal of the American Medical Association* 262:365-369.

Sarason, I., J. Johnson and J. Siegel. 1978. Assessing the impact of life change. *Journal of Consulting and Clinical Psychology* 46:932-946.

Schimmel, D., J. Sullivan and D. Mrad. 1989. Suicide prevention in the federal prison system. In D. Lester, ed., *Suicide '89*. Denver: American Association of Suicidology.

Schneider, A.Z., N. Kordas and P. Herndon. 1990. The Impact of Crisis Intervention on Suicide Potential and Hospitalization of Juvenile Detainees. In D. Lester, ed., *Suicide '90*. Denver: American Association of Suicidology.

Segest, E. 1987. Police custody. *Journal of Forensic Sciences* 32:1694-1703.

Severson, M.M. 1991. Update — suicide prevention in detention facilities. In D. Lester, ed., *Suicide '91*. Denver: American Association of Suicidology.

Sherman, L.G. and P.C. Morschauser. 1989. Screening for suicide risk in inmates. *Psychiatric Quarterly* 60:119-138.

Sloane, B.C. 1973. Suicide attempters in the District of Columbia prison system. *Omega* 4:37-50.

Smialek, J. and W. Spitz. 1978. Deaths behind bars. *Journal of the American Medical Association* 240:2563-2564.

Smith, R. 1984. Deaths in prison. *British Medical Journal* 288:208-212.

Sovronsky, H.R. and I. Shapiro. 1989. The New York State model suicide prevention training program for local corrections officers. *Psychiatric Quarterly* 90:139-149.

Spellman, A. and B. Heyne. 1989. Suicide? Accident? Predictable? Avoidable? *Psychiatric Quarterly* 60:173-183.

Spencer, J. 1989. Aboriginal deaths in custody. *Australian and New Zealand Journal of Psychiatry* 23:164-165.

Sperbeck, D.J. and R.R. Parlour. 1986. Screening and suicidal prisoners. *Corrective and Social Psychiatry* 32(3):95-98.

Stack, S. 1990. Media Impacts on Suicide. In D. Lester, ed., *Current Concepts of Suicide*. Philadelphia: The Charles Press.

Stone, W.E. 1984. Jail suicide. *Corrections Today* 46(6):84-87.

Stone, W.E. 1984. Means of the cause of death in Texas jail suicides, 1986-1988. *American Jails* 4(1):50-53.

Taylor, P.J. and J. Gunn. 1984. Violence and psychosis. *British Medical Journal* 288:1945-1946.

Toch, H. 1975. *Men in Crisis*. Chicago: Aldine.

Topp, D. 1979. Suicide in prison. *British Journal of Psychiatry* 134:24-27.

Tracy, F.J. 1972. Suicide and suicide prevention in New York City prisons. *Probation and Parole* 4:20-29.

Vogel, R. and M. Wolfersdorf. 1987. Staff response to the suicide of psychiatric inpatients. *Crisis* 8:178-184.

Walsh, B.W. and P.M. Rosen. 1988. *Self-mutilation*. New York: Guilford.

Whitmer, G. 1980. From hospitals to jails. *American Journal of Orthopsychiatry* 50:65-75.

Whittemore, K. 1970. *Ten Centers*. Atlanta: Lullwater.

Wicks, R.J. 1972. Suicide prevention. *Federal Probation* 36(3):29-31.

Wicks, R.J. 1974. *Correctional Psychology*. San Francisco, Canfield Press.

Wiggs, J.W. 1989. Prison rape and suicide. *Journal of the American Medical Association* 262:3403.

Wilmotte, J.N. and J. Plat-Mendelwicz. 1973. Epidemiology of Suicidal Behavior in One Thousand Belgian Prisoners. In B. Danto, ed., *Jailhouse Blues*. Orchard Lake, MI: Epic.

Winfree, L.T. 1987. Toward understanding state-level jail mortality. *Justice Quarterly* 4:51-71.

Winfree, L.T. 1988. Rethinking American jail death rates. *Policy Studies Review* 7(3):641-659.

Wool, R.J. and E. Dooley. 1987. A study of attempted suicides in prisons. *Medicine, Science and the Law* 27:297-301.

Woolley, L.F. and A.H. Eichert. 1941. Notes on the problems of suicide and escape. *American Journal of Psychiatry* 98:110-118.

Zung, W.W. 1965. A self-rating depression scale. *Archives of General Psychiatry* 12:63-70.